Upper Columbia Basin Network
Integrated Water Quality Annual Report 2009-2011
Whitman Mission National Historic Site (WHMI)

Natural Resource Technical Report NPS/UCBN/NRTR—2012/580

Eric Starkey

Aquatic Biologist
Upper Columbia Basin Network Inventory and Monitoring Program
105 E. 2nd St.
Suite #7
Moscow, ID 83843

June 2012

U.S. Department of the Interior
National Park Service
Natural Resource Stewardship and Science
Fort Collins, Colorado

The National Park Service, Natural Resource Stewardship and Science office in Fort Collins, Colorado publishes a range of reports that address natural resource topics of interest and applicability to a broad audience in the National Park Service and others in natural resource management, including scientists, conservation and environmental constituencies, and the public.

The Natural Resource Technical Report Series is used to disseminate results of scientific studies in the physical, biological, and social sciences for both the advancement of science and the achievement of the National Park Service mission. The series provides contributors with a forum for displaying comprehensive data that are often deleted from journals because of page limitations.

All manuscripts in the series receive the appropriate level of peer review to ensure that the information is scientifically credible, technically accurate, appropriately written for the intended audience, and designed and published in a professional manner.

Data in this report were collected and analyzed using methods based on established, peer-reviewed protocols and were analyzed and interpreted within the guidelines of the protocols.

Views, statements, findings, conclusions, recommendations, and data in this report do not necessarily reflect views and policies of the National Park Service, U.S. Department of the Interior. Mention of trade names or commercial products does not constitute endorsement or recommendation for use by the U.S. Government.

This report is available from the Upper Columbia Basin Network (http://www.nature.nps.gov/im/units/ucbn/) and the Natural Resource Publications Management website (http://www.nature.nps.gov/publications/nrpm/).

Please cite this publication as:

Starkey, E. N. 2012. Upper Columbia Basin Network integrated water quality annual report 2009-2011: Whitman Mission National Historic Site (WHMI). Natural Resource Technical Report NPS/UCBN/NRTR—2012/580. National Park Service, Fort Collins, Colorado.

NPS 371/114303, June 2012

Contents

Contents (continued)

Figures

Figures (continued)

Tables

Tables (continued)

Appendices

Executive Summary

The mission of the National Park Service is "to conserve unimpaired the natural and cultural resources and values of the national park system for the enjoyment of this and future generations" (NPS 1999). To uphold this goal, the Director of the NPS approved the Natural Resource Challenge to encourage national parks to focus on the preservation of the nation's natural heritage through science, natural resource inventories, and expanded resource monitoring (NPS 1999). Through the Challenge, 270 parks in the national park system were organized into 32 inventory and monitoring networks. The Upper Columbia Basin Network (UCBN) is comprised of 8 national park sites located in Idaho, Montana, Oregon, and Washington.

The UCBN has identified 14 priority park vital signs, indicators of ecosystem health, which represent a broad suite of ecological phenomena operating across multiple temporal and spatial scales. The intent of the network is to monitor a balanced and integrated "package" of vital signs that meets the needs of current park management, but will also be able to accommodate unanticipated environmental conditions in the future. Water quality is a particularly high priority vital sign for six of the nine UCBN parks. The UCBN contains more than 34 rivers, streams, ponds, and reservoirs. Unlike many National Parks that are large and often encompass entire watersheds, most UCBN parks and water bodies are small and embedded in large watersheds with diverse land use.

This annual report details the status of key indicators of water quality obtained from monitoring that occurred in Whitman Mission National Historic Site (WHMI) in 2009, 2010, and 2011. WHMI natural resource staff monitored Mill Creek in 2009, Doan Creek in 2010, and Mill Creek again in 2011. For more information regarding the status of Mill Creek in 2008 (see Starkey 2009). All data was collected following methods detailed in the UCBN integrated water quality monitoring protocol (Starkey et al. 2008). The UCBN Integrated Water Quality Monitoring Protocol was formally peer-reviewed and approved for implementation in August 2009. This protocol can be found on the UCBN website at: http://science.nature.nps.gov/im/units/ucbn/reports/index.cfm#IWQ_Mon. Benthic macroinvertebrates were collected by the United States Forest Service- PACFISH/INFISH Biological Opinion (PIBO) according to their peer reviewed protocol during the UCBN's monitoring of stream channel characteristics and riparian condition in 2011. The UCBN's peer reviewed stream channel characteristics and riparian condition protocols can also be found on the UCBN's website listed above.

Water chemistry and macroinvertebrate results indicate that Doan and Mill Creek are in fair condition, with the primary concerns being elevated water temperatures, low dissolved oxygen levels, and pH levels above established thresholds. The status of water quality for Doan and Mill Creek relative to state regulatory thresholds is given in the summary tables on the following page.

Standard UCBN water quality monitoring is conducted on a 3 year rotating panel; however WHMI natural resource staff has decided to monitor every year. As a result, conditions in Mill Creek will be re-evaluated in 2012 and again in 2014. Doan Creek will be re-evaluated in 2013.

Note that several of the appendices in this report are primarily intended for UCBN internal reference. In addition, some appendices serve as hard copies of quality assurance/quality control procedures performed during data processing.

Doan Creek Water Chemistry Summary 2010

Measure	Current Condition (April-November, 2010)	State DOE Thresholds[a]	% Exceedance[b]
Temperature (*MDMT, **MDAT)	* MDMT= 20.3 °C ** MDAT= 17.8 °C	***7-DADMax <16 °C	46%
Specific conductance (mean)	501.0 µS/cm	N/A	N/A
Dissolved oxygen (mean daily min)	8.3 mg/L	>9.5 mg/L Minimum Daily Minimum	96%
pH (mean daily max)	8.0 pH Units	8.5 pH Units, Max (0.5 units human caused variation)	0%
pH (mean daily min)	7.9 pH Units	6.5 pH Units, Min (0.5 units human caused variation)	0%
Turbidity (mean daily max)	36.1 NTU	< 5 NTU increase above background when background NTU < 50, < 10% increase when background NTU > 50	Insufficient data
E. coli	110 cfu/100 ml	No state standard for E. coli. In adjacent states, individual samples <406/100ml are generally considered acceptable	0%

Mill Creek Water Chemistry Summary 2011

Measure	Current Condition (June-November, 2011)	State DOE Thresholds[a]	% Exceedance[b]
Temperature (*MDMT, **MDAT)	* MDMT= 24.5 °C ** MDAT= 21.7 °C	***7-DADMax <16 °C	72%
Specific conductance (mean)	278.7 µS/cm	N/A	N/A
Dissolved oxygen (mean daily min)	7.1 mg/l	>9.5 mg/l Minimum Daily Minimum	100%
pH (mean daily max)	8.7 pH Units	8.5 pH Units, Max (0.5 units human caused variation)	19%
pH (mean daily min)	7.6 pH Units	6.5 pH Units, Min (0.5 units human caused variation)	0%
Turbidity (mean daily max)	Insufficient data due to poor data quality	< 5 NTU increase above background when background NTU < 50, < 10% increase when background NTU > 50	Insufficient data
E. coli	130 cfu/100 ml	No state standard for E. coli. In adjacent states, individual samples <406/100ml are generally considered acceptable	0%

*MDMT – Maximum Daily Maximum Temperature, **MDAT – Maximum Daily Average Temperature, ***7-DADMax –7 DayAverage Daily Maximum Temperature, [a] Criteria established for Class AA , [b] Proportion of samples above water quality standard.

0-5% exceedance	
5-25% exceedance	
>25% exceedance	

Acknowledgments

Funding for this project was provided through the National Park Service Natural Resource Challenge and the Servicewide Inventory and Monitoring Program. Special thanks to Roger Trick for his commitment to water quality monitoring in WHMI.

Introduction and Background

Water resources have been identified as a high priority vital sign for the Upper Columbia Basin Network (UCBN). These resources are used by many riparian, migratory, and terrestrial organisms in the Network, and have intrinsic value as places of natural beauty and recreation (Garrett et al. 2007). Reflecting this priority, the Water Resources Division (WRD) of the NPS provides a separate source of funding each fiscal year to the UCBN to accomplish water quality monitoring. In June 2011 the UCBN began its third year of integrated water quality monitoring in Mill Creek. Note that WHMI natural resource staff has committed to water quality monitoring within the park on a yearly basis and rotates monitoring between Mill and Doan Creek. In June 2009 WHMI conducted monitoring in Doan Creek and was the first assessment of this stream using the UCBN protocol.

Water resources in the semi-arid West have been strongly affected by human activity, and many UCBN streams and rivers are listed by states as impaired for one or more parameters. Most UCBN water bodies and many aquatic resources such as migratory fish are strongly influenced by activities in the larger watersheds outside park boundaries. Understanding the current status of freshwater ecosystems will help guide management and restoration efforts, and provide insight into ecosystem change in a landscape with a shifting climate and dynamic human influences.

During the process of prioritizing vital signs to monitor in UCBN parks in 2005, water quality was identified as a high priority vital sign (Garrett et al. 2007). When asked what aspects of water quality were important to monitor, resource managers identified the sampling of macroinvertebrate assemblages within UCBN water bodies as the top water quality monitoring priority. Secondary priorities included baseline sampling of water chemistry parameters, characterization of channel morphology, and information on water quantity. Channel morphology and riparian vegetation are addressed in separate monitoring protocols which were also implemented at WHMI in 2011.

The objectives of the UCBN Integrated Water Quality Monitoring Protocol are documenting the aquatic macroinvertebrate assemblage composition and baseline water chemistry parameters. Aquatic macroinvertebrate assemblages have strong effects on freshwater ecosystem processes and represent an important trophic linkage between primary producers and fishes. Measures of macroinvertebrate assemblage composition and structure have been frequently used as water quality indicators because these assemblages integrate the effects of point and non-point source pollutants over spatial-temporal scales and can be used to answer many management questions. Also, macroinvertebrates are more cost-effective to sample than other biota or many water chemistry parameters.

Water chemistry and temperature have strong effects on aquatic biota. Consequently, direct and indirect human alteration of stream water quality is associated with altered biotic communities and ecosystem processes. Because of the direct relationship between water chemistry and biota, water chemistry is typically a central component of any water quality monitoring program. More recently, monitoring of stream water temperatures has increased in the Pacific Northwest, because of concerns over cold-water fish habitat (primarily salmonid fishes), the recognized influence of land- and water-use on stream temperature regime, and the need for baseline temperature information to monitor the effects of climate change. National Park Service (NPS) Water Resource Division (WRD) has identified a suite of four "core water quality parameters": temperature, specific conductance, pH, and dissolved oxygen, which are critical to understanding baseline conditions in aquatic habitats. The UCBN added turbidity as a parameter to measure because turbidity is listed as a source of impairment in several UCBN park streams.

Well articulated desired future condition statements have not yet been developed for water quality in UCBN parks. However, the mission statements for the NPS as a whole and for the individual parks clearly state the intent "to conserve unimpaired the natural and cultural resources and values of the national park system for the enjoyment of this and future generations" (NPS 1999). Water quality is a particularly important resource with nationally recognized merit. It is assumed that desired future conditions for all UCBN parks will include clean streams, rivers, and lakes free of human health concerns that provide visitors with recreational and scenic experiences. Monitoring macroinvertebrate assemblage composition and structure, and core water quality parameters will directly measure the water characteristics most important to park mission, visitor experience, and desired future conditions.

Objectives

The overarching programmatic goal of the UCBN integrated water quality monitoring program is to obtain information that will aid in informed management decisions pertaining to improved water quality within UCBN parks. Park managers have committed to improving the water quality of impaired waters by adopting the NPS Government Performance Results Act (GPRA) goal (Ia4) that streams and rivers managed by NPS will meet State and Federal water quality standards (NPS 2000).

Given this goal, it should be noted that in 2008 Doan Creek was listed as a category 4A water for temperature. Category 4A means that it has a pollution problem, but has total maximum daily load (TMDL) being actively implemented to remedy issues. In addition, in 2008 Mill Creek was listed as a category 4A water for pollution problems related to: temperature, pH, fecal coliform, and dissolved oxygen.

Given the lack of available data on water quality in UCBN parks, the following fundamental questions drive much of the UCBN's inquiry into water quality:

- Are the core water quality parameters of streams in the UCBN with established Total Maximum Daily Loads (TMDLs) selected for sampling improving over time?
- What is the status and long-term trend of core water quality parameters (temperature, pH, conductivity, dissolved oxygen, and turbidity) in UCBN streams selected for sampling?
- What is the status and long term trend in aquatic macroinvertebrate abundance and assemblage composition in selected UCBN streams?
- Do aquatic macroinvertebrate assemblages sampled within UCBN streams indicate polluted or otherwise impaired water quality?
- Do aquatic macroinvertebrate assemblages sampled within UCBN streams indicate "pristine" or "reference" conditions according to regional criteria established by the Environmental Protection Agency (EPA) and the states of Idaho, Oregon, Montana, and Washington?

In light of these questions and the broader goals outlined above, water quality monitoring in the UCBN addresses the following specific measurable monitoring objectives:

- Determine status and long term trend in key water quality parameters for selected streams within UCBN park units.
- Determine status and trend in aquatic macroinvertebrate abundance, assemblage composition, and functional feeding group composition in wadeable streams within the UCBN.

Study Area

Doan Creek- Whitman Mission National Historic Site (WHMI)

The segment of Doan Creek within the park is in the Walla Walla River subbasin in Hydrologic Unit Code (HUC 6)170701020204 (United States Geologic Survey [USGS]), Lower Mill Creek subwatershed, in Walla Walla County, Washington (Figures 1 and 2; Appendix B). "Doan Creek is a left bank, spring-fed tributary of Mill Creek. Doan Creek originates three miles east of the WHMI and passes through a private airport, a former dairy, and agricultural land before entering the site at the northeastern boundary. From there, Doan Creek runs through a restored channel continuing west along the northern boundary until joining with Mill Creek. An irrigation water pumping station draws water out of Doan Creek into the irrigation ditch that supplies water to the park and to two downstream irrigators (Bell and Hinson 2009)." Restoration of the Doan Creek channel and riparian area began in 2004 with some stream channel modification work occurring in 2008 and again in 2011. See Bell and Hinson 2009 for a more detailed description of modifications.

The WHMI watershed is approximately 276 square km (107 square miles) and consists of several land cover types (Bell and Hinson 2009). According to Bell and Hinson 2009, WHMI's watershed is primarily dominated by agriculture (73.98%) with a substantial proportion of the watershed being classified as developed (11.16%) or rural development (8.16%). The remaining land was classified as native and non-native dominated grass, shrub, and tree dominated vegetation (6.93%). The majority of this land cover type was found higher in the watershed.

Designated beneficial uses for Doan Creek include Salmonid spawning, rearing, and migration; primary contact recreation; domestic, industrial, and agricultural water supply; stock watering; wildlife habitat; harvesting; commerce and navigation; boating; and aesthetic values (WA Admin. Code 2011, 173-201A-600 [through 8/1/03]). In addition, the segment of Doan Creek within the National Park boundary has the following designated beneficial uses: core summer salmonid habitat; and extraordinary primary contact recreation (WA Admin Code 2011, 173-201A-600 [through 8/1/03]). It is important to note that the segment of Doan Creek, immediately upstream of the park is considered a "class A" waterbody and has less stringent water quality standards than exist for the stream as it flows through the park (designated "class AA") (WA Admin. Code 2011, 173-201A-600 [through 8/1/03], Stohr et al. 2007).

Threats to water resources in WHMI have been identified as: agricultural chemical use, over allocation of irrigation water, and a private airfield 3 miles upstream (Garrett et al. 2007). In 2008, Doan Creek was listed as a category 4A impaired water for temperature (Washington Department of Ecology 2008). The category 4A designation means that it has a pollution problem, but has total maximum daily loads (TMDL) being actively implemented to reduce pollution. Information about the current TMDLs and recent water quality conditions within the Walla Walla watershed can be found in: Joy et al. 2006, Baldwin and Stohr 2007, Joy et al. 2007, Stohr et al. 2007, and Baldwin et al. 2008. Additional information specific to Doan Creek can be found in: UCBN's water quality monitoring report for WHMI (Starkey 2009), Natural Resource Condition Assessment: Whitman Mission National Historic Site (Bell and Hinson 2009), Baseline Water Quality Data- Inventory and Analysis WHMI (NPS 1997), Doan Creek

Restoration Project Phase 1 & 2 Final Report (WWCCD 2008), and Whitman Mission National Historic Site-Doan Creek Restoration Project Environmental Assessment (NPS 2005).
In 2010 the Hydrolab was deployed approximately 100 m upstream from the mouth of Doan Creek (i.e. confluence with Mill Creek).(Figure 1 and 3; Appendices A and C). This location was chosen primarily due to adequate water depth throughout summer months and lack of suitable pools throughout the remainder of the park.

The macroinvertebrate sample reach on Doan Creek (sampled in 2011) coincides with the stream channel characteristics and riparian condition monitoring reach (see Appendix C for GPS waypoint). See the 2011 WHMI stream channel characteristics and riparian condition annual report for a detailed reach description.

Figure 1. Doan Creek looking downstream towards water quality monitoring station #01 (red circle) and confluence with Mill Creek.

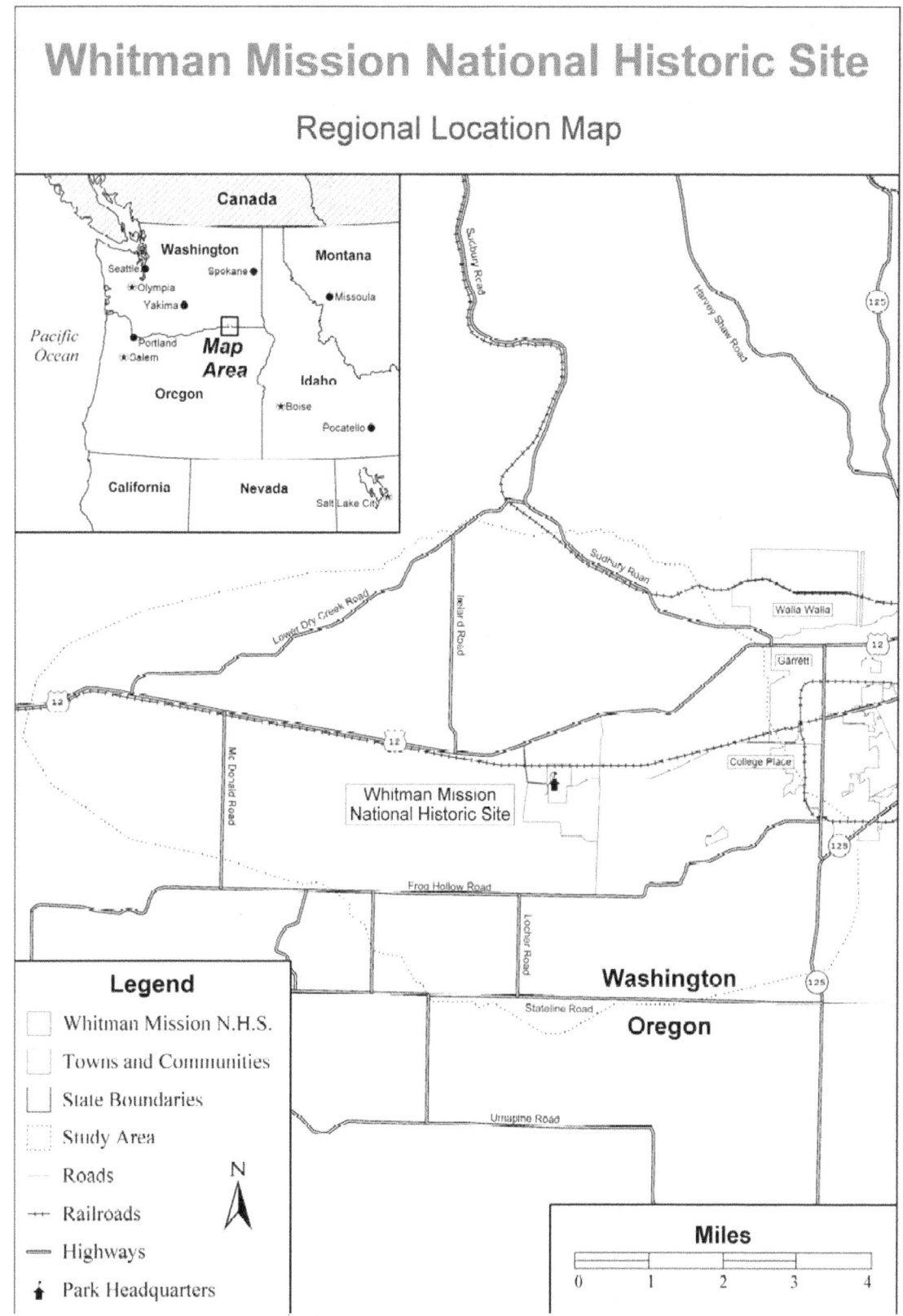

Figure 2. Whitman Mission National Historic Site regional map (NPS 1997).

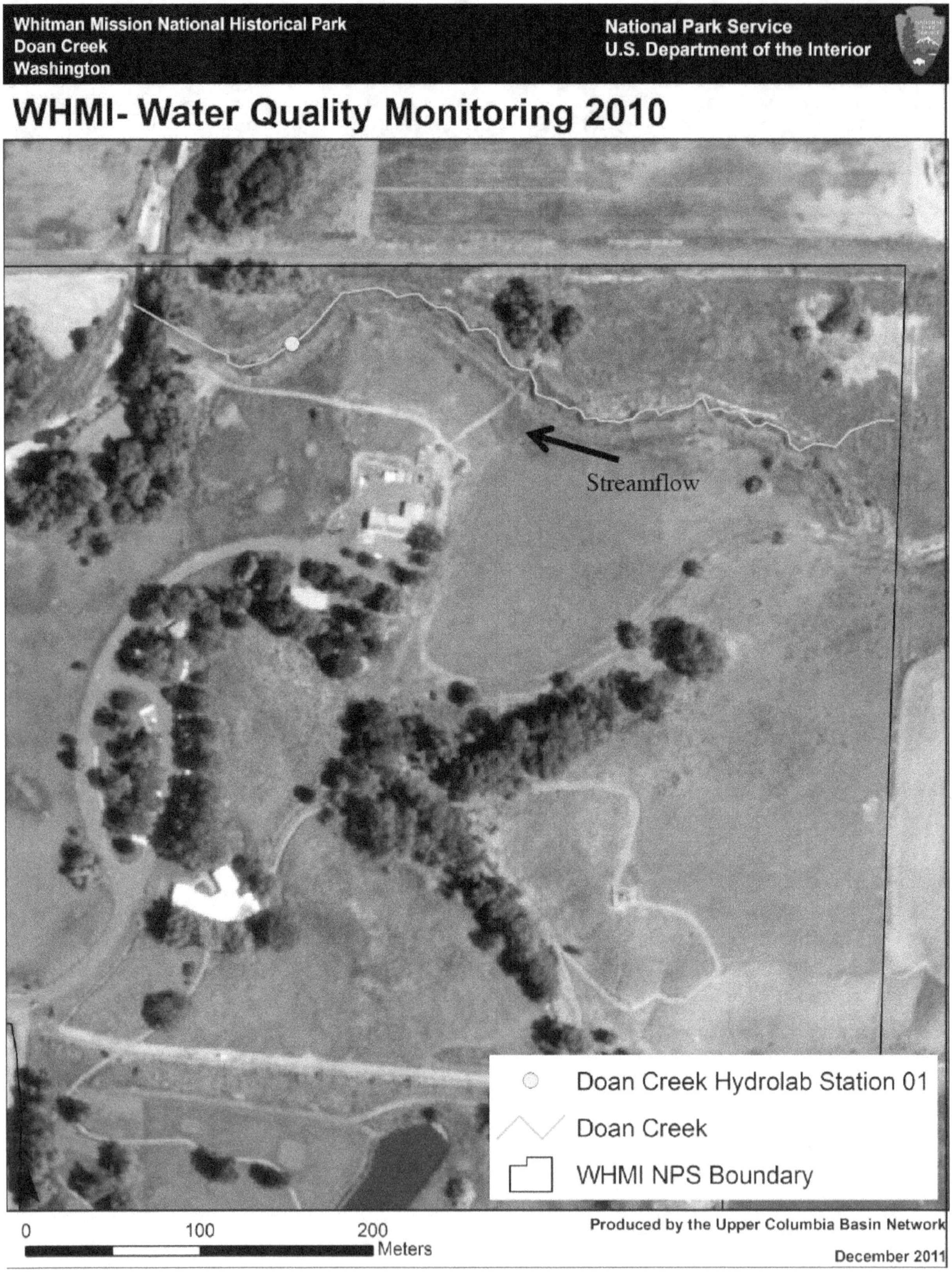

WHMI- Water Quality Monitoring 2010

Streamflow

○   Doan Creek Hydrolab Station 01

/\/   Doan Creek

⬜   WHMI NPS Boundary

0   100   200
                    Meters

Produced by the Upper Columbia Basin Network

December 2011

Figure 3. Water quality monitoring location in Doan Creek 2010.

Figure 4. Water quality monitoring location on Mill Creek 2011.

Mill Creek- Whitman Mission National Historic Site (WHMI)

The segment of Mill Creek within the park is in the Walla Walla River subbasin in Hydrologic Unit Code (HUC 6)170701020204 (United States Geologic Survey [USGS]), Lower Mill Creek subwatershed, in Walla Walla County, Washington (Figures 2, 4, and 5; Appendix B). "Mill Creek originates on the western slopes of the Blue Mountains, in southeastern Washington, at an elevation of 5,500 feet (USACE 1995b). It flows for 15 miles in a relatively deep and narrow canyon, through mountainous terrain, and then enters an alluvial fan a few miles east of the City of Walla Walla. Mill Creek flows through the northern corner of the WHMI property where it collects streamflow from Doan Creek then enters the Walla Walla River about ½ mile west of WHMI (Bell and Hinson 2009)."

The WHMI watershed is approximately 276 square km (107 square miles) and consists of several land cover types (Bell and Hinson 2009). According to Bell and Hinson 2009, WHMI's watershed is primarily dominated by agriculture (73.98%) with a substantial proportion of the watershed being classified as developed (11.16%) or rural development (8.16%). The remaining land was classified as native and non-native dominated grass, shrub, and tree dominated vegetation (6.93%). The majority of this land cover type was found higher in the watershed.

Designated beneficial uses for Mill Creek (from mouth to 13th street bridge in Walla Walla) include rearing, and migration; secondary contact recreation; industrial, and agricultural water supply; stock watering; wildlife habitat; harvesting; commerce and navigation; boating; and aesthetic values (WA Admin. Code 2011, 173-201A-600 [through 8/1/03]). However, as defined within the Washington administrative code, the segment of Mill Creek within the National Park should also be protected for the designated uses of: core summer salmonid habitat and extraordinary primary contact recreation (2011, 173-201A-600 [through 8/1/03]). It is important to note that the segment of Mill Creek, immediately upstream and downstream of the park (from mouth to 13th street bridge in Walla Walla) is considered a "class B" waterbody and has less stringent water quality standards than exist for the stream as it flows through the park (designated "class AA") (WA Admin. Code 2011, 173-201A-600 [through 8/1/03], Stohr et al. 2007).

Threats to water resources in WHMI have been identified as: agricultural chemical use, over allocation of irrigation water, and a private airfield 3 miles upstream (Garrett et al. 2007). In 2008, Mill Creek was listed as a category 4A impaired water for temperature, pH, fecal coliform, and dissolved oxygen (Washington Department of Ecology 2008). The category 4A designation means that it has a pollution problem, but has total maximum daily loads (TMDL) being actively implemented to reduce pollution. Information about the current TMDLs and recent water quality conditions within the Walla Walla watershed can be found in: Joy et al. 2006, Baldwin and Stohr 2007, Joy et al. 2007, Stohr et al. 2007, and Baldwin et al. 2008. Additional information specific to Mill Creek can be found in: UCBN's water quality monitoring report for WHMI (Starkey 2009), Natural Resource Condition Assessment: Whitman Mission National Historic Site (Bell and Hinson 2009), Baseline Water Quality Data- Inventory and Analysis WHMI (NPS 1997), and Mill Creek Master Plan, Main Report, volume 1 and 2 (USACE 1995a, USACE 1995b).

In 2009 and 2011 the Hydrolab was deployed approximately 150 m downstream from the railroad bridge/northern park boundary (Figure 4 and 5; Appendices A and C). This location was the same monitoring location as in 2008 and was chosen primarily due to adequate water depth throughout summer months and consistent flow.

The macroinvertebrate sample reach (sampled in 2011) on Mill Creek coincides with the stream channel characteristics and riparian condition monitoring reach (see Appendix C for GPS waypoint). See the 2011 WHMI stream channel characteristics and riparian condition annual report for a detailed reach description.

Figure 5. Mill Creek looking downstream towards water quality monitoring station #01.

Methods

Water Chemistry

Since the last water quality annual report was issued for WHMI (Starkey 2009), continuous water quality monitors (HACH, MS5 Hydrolabs) were deployed from June 15th to November 24th 2009 in Mill Creek; and April 20th to November 19th 2010 in Doan Creek; and again in Mill Creek from June 22nd to November 8th 2011. Monitors were deployed at index sites to estimate the status, variability, and long-term trends in core parameters. The core parameters measured were water temperature, dissolved oxygen, pH, specific conductance, and turbidity. These core parameters were measured hourly and the instrument serviced monthly throughout the deployment period. Each monitor was deployed in a location that was representative of conditions in the park, logistically feasible to access, and relatively secure from vandalism and high flows. A cross-section survey was conducted to aid in the determination of Hydrolab site selection. For more information on the UCBN water chemistry sampling design see Starkey et al. (2008). It should be noted that 2011 represented the first year the Hydrolab was powered via an external power supply (solar panel/battery). Gaps in monitoring prior to 2011 occurred primarily due to loss of battery power. In 2009 and 2011 gaps in monitoring (June/July) were due to dissolved oxygen sensor failure and subsequent repair of Hydrolab #095.

Quality Assurance/Quality Control (QA/QC):

Quality assurance and quality control for multiprobe data collection are covered in detail in SOP #12 (Starkey et al. 2008). Basic procedures adhere to the guidelines established in Part B lite (Irwin 2008); the National Coastal Assessment Quality Assurance Project Plan 2001-2004 (U.S. EPA 2001); the Laboratory Methods Manual-Estuaries, Volume 1: Biological and Physical Analyses (U.S. EPA 1995); and Rapid Bioassessment Protocols for Use in Streams and Wadeable Rivers (Barbour et al. 1999).

General quality assurance and quality control methods for UCBN water quality multiprobe calibration and data downloads include the following:

- Representative multiprobe sample locations are determined by using a cross-section and stream segment survey. Each site is re-assessed for representativeness at the start and end each sample year.

- The UCBN follows pre-established maximum acceptable differences for field instrument calibration and QC checks. If the multiprobe readings are outside of the maximum acceptable differences, the multiprobe is removed for non-routine maintenance.

- When calibrating the multiprobe, values of known standard solutions are measured pre and post calibration, to help determine if the instrument's measurements have "drifted." In addition, repeated measures of these solutions are used to determine the repeatability of multiprobe measures.

- All multiprobe data is visually checked for outliers and QC issues immediately following the download of data. QC issues indicated by the data may include: wiper parking, defective sensors, power supply problems, and other anomalies affecting data quality.

- Quantitative and qualitative terms that describe how accurate data need to be in order to meet project objectives are discussed in detail in SOP #12 Starkey et al. 2008 and Appendix D in this report. NPS WRD lists the following data quality objectives as necessary for water chemistry data: target population, representativeness, completeness, data comparability, measurement sensitivity and detection limits, measurement precision as repeatability, and measurement systematic error/bias.

More detailed QA/QC for water quality multiprobes is contained in SOP #6 and 12, Starkey et al. 2008.

Discharge
Water discharge was determined by data available from the United States Geological Survey (USGS) real time gauging sites. For Mill Creek, the closest gage is at Walla Walla WA, #14015000. This data was used to aid in the interpretation of continuous water chemistry data collected in Mill Creek June – November 2009 and 2011. No USGS gauging station exists on Doan Creek.

Macroinvertebrates
On both Doan and Mill Creeks, macroinvertebrates were collected at designated sample reaches (1 on Mill Creek, 1 on Doan Creek) by the United States Forest Service- PACFISH/INFISH Biological Opinion (PIBO) Effectiveness Monitoring Program during the assessment of stream channel characteristics in 2011. This assessment was completed as part of the UCBNs stream channel characteristics monitoring protocol. Macroinvertebrates were collected from 8 fast water habitats (riffles, runs) in each sample reach. These 8 samples were combined for a single composite sample per reach. For more information on the PIBO macroinvertebrate sampling design see Heitke et al. (2008).

Coliform
At the request of the park, coliform samples were collected to determine baseline counts for total coliform and *E. coli*. Note that coliform sampling is not routinely performed as part of the Integrated Water Quality Protocol. Samples were drawn from both Doan and Mill Creeks near the water quality monitoring stations on August 3rd, 2011. Samples were chilled and transported to the Walla Walla County Health Department in Walla Walla, WA for analysis.

Results

Doan Creek- 2010

Water Chemistry:

Cross Section Survey:
A cross section survey was conducted at the proposed multiprobe deployment location to evaluate if the site was reasonably representative of stream conditions throughout the park. As suggested by the water resource division the UCBN judges overall representativeness primarily on the basis of specific conductance (Starkey et al. 2008).

The 2010 deployment location provided adequate water depth throughout the field season, was easily accessible, and was away from heavily trafficked access points. In addition, there are limited other deployment locations along the creek due to lack of deep pools.

A one way analysis of variance (ANOVA) test was conducted to evaluate representativeness (R v2.12.0). Results of the ANOVA showed that there was no significant difference for specific conductance among the transects and the deployment location in April $F_{(4,33)}=2.65$, $p > 0.05$ and a significant difference in November $F_{(4,30)}= 9.57$, $p < 0.05$.

To determine where the difference in representativeness occurred, a post hoc Tukey's test was conducted (R v2.12.0). Relative to specific conductance, results of the Tukey's test for the cross section conducted in November indicates that the deployment location was significantly different from transects 3 and 4 (Figure 7).

In summary, the deployment location was shown to be representative when monitoring began in April (Figure 6). The November cross section survey indicated the monitoring station may not have been representative of conditions near transects 3 and 4; however, the monitoring location was within one of the largest and deepest available pools, and represents the best location suitable for permanent deployment.

In the future, this location will likely remain the best option for long term deployment of the water quality monitor.

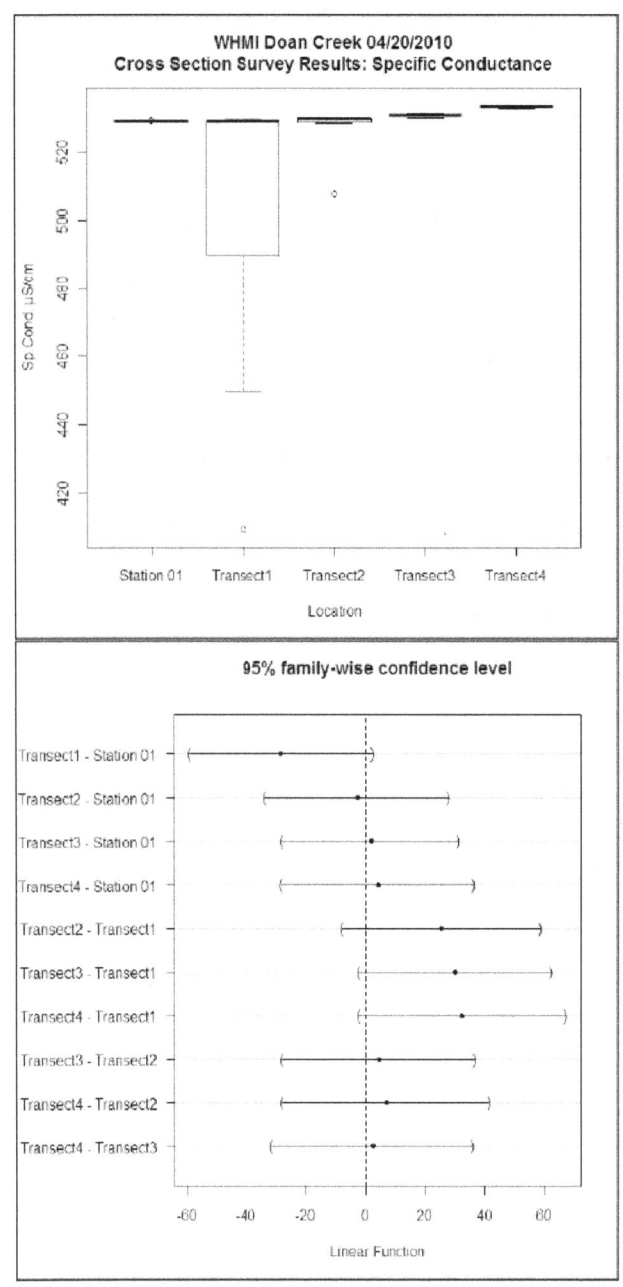

Figure 6. April 2010 cross section survey of Doan Creek, box plot of specific conductance and plot of 95% family-wise confidence level.Note that "Station 01" is the location of multiprobe deployment and transects progress downstream (1-4).

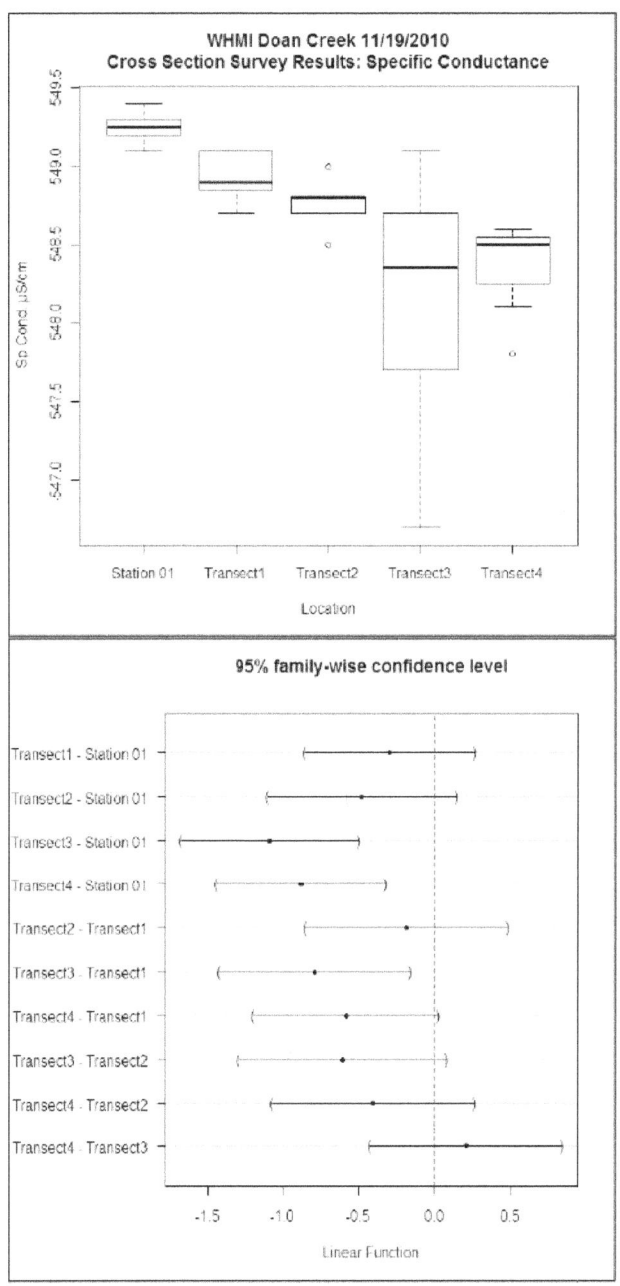

Figure 7. November 2010 cross section survey of Doan Creek, box plot of specific conductance and plot of 95% family-wise confidence level. Note that "Station 01" is the location of multiprobe deployment and transects progress upstream (1-4).

Status:
Condition of core water quality parameters along with the corresponding state Department of Ecology (WADOE) regulatory threshold are given in Table 1. The primary concerns are elevated water temperatures, low dissolved oxygen levels and their effects on native fish and other cold water biota. Each parameter is discussed in further detail below.

Table 1. Vital sign summary table for water chemistry in Doan Creek April-November, 2010

Doan Creek Water Chemistry Summary 2010

Measure	Current Condition (April-November, 2010)	State DOE Thresholds[a]	% Exceedance[c]
Temperature (*MDMT, **MDAT)	* MDMT= 20.3 °C ** MDAT= 17.8 °C	***7-DADMax <16 °C	46%
Specific conductance (mean)	501.0 µS/cm	N/A	N/A
Dissolved oxygen (mean daily min)	8.3 mg/L	>9.5 mg/L Minimum Daily Minimum	96%
pH (mean daily max)	8.0 pH Units	8.5 pH Units, Max (0.5 units human caused variation)	0%
pH (mean daily min)	7.9 pH Units	6.5 pH Units, Min (0.5 units human caused variation)	0%
Turbidity (mean daily max)	36.1 NTU	< 5 NTU increase above background when background NTU < 50, < 10% increase when background NTU > 50	Insufficient data
E. coli	110 cfu/100 ml	Geometric mean of samples < 200 cfu/100 ml, < 10% of the samples can exceed 400 cfu/100 mL [b]	0%

*MDMT – Maximum Daily Maximum Temperature, **MDAT – Maximum Daily Average Temperature, ***7-DADMax –7 DayAverage Daily Maximum Temperature, [a] Criteria established for Class AA , [b] Secondary contact recreational use critera, [c] Proportion of samples above water quality standard

0-5% exceedance	
5-25% exceedance	
>25% exceedance	

- *Temperature:*
  The maximum daily maximum temperature (MDMT) was 20.3 °C and the maximum daily average temperature (MDAT) was 17.8 °C. Water temperature routinely exceeded (46%) the standard designated for "class AA core summer salmonid habitat" (7-DADMax <16°C), but only exceeded the "class A salmonid, spawning, rearing and migration" standard (7-DADMax <17.5°C) during 19% of observations (Baldwin and Stohr 2007). When compared to either "class AA" or "A" standards, these data suggest the need for an increase in stream shading via riparian vegetation within the watershed. In addition, given that streamflow during the summer is maintained by ground water, upstream withdrawals may be impacting stream temperatures by reducing streamflow. Our data reinforces basin-wide temperature concerns as discussed in the Walla Walla Watershed Temperature Total Maximum Daily Load (TMDL)- Water Quality Improvement Report (Baldwin and Stohr 2007). Figure 8 shows the daily maximum and mean daily temperatures in Doan Creek from April-November 2010. Table 2 lists the data rating/grade for each deployment period (monthly interval). These standard USGS ratings are based on the degree of sensor fouling and drift

encountered during each deployment period (Wagner et al. 2006; Starkey et al. 2008). Data grades less than "excellent" were due in large part to sensor fouling and error when reading the NIST thermometer during the assessment of fouling/drift.

Water temperatures are of particular interest in Doan Creek, given that its designated uses include: Salmonid spawning, rearing, and migration; and core summer salmonid habitat. Implications of elevated water temperatures may include decreased salmonid recruitment, decreased salmonid health, and potential shifts in fish and benthic macroinvertebrate communities (Vannote and Sweeney 1980; McCullough 1999). It is also important to note that elevated water temperatures have the capacity to reduce the total concentration of dissolved oxygen (i.e., there is an inverse relationship between water temperature and dissolved oxygen; Figure 10), thereby impacting aquatic biota.

Maintaining water temperatures suitable for naturally occurring species in Doan Creek will depend on riparian and stream channel conditions basin-wide. For this reason cooperation with other agencies, stakeholders, and adjacent landowners will be critical for improving water temperature. The steps being taken by WHMI to restore their segment of Doan Creek and provide year round stream flow is progress towards meeting temperature targets.

- *Specific Conductance:*
Specific conductance ranged from 213.0 to 589.9 μS/cm, with an average specific conductance of 501.0 μS/cm. The steady increase in specific conductance from mid May to September shown in Figure 9 reflects the decrease in surface flow throughout the summer. Table 3 shows the data rating/grade for each deployment period (monthly interval). These standard USGS ratings are based on the degree of sensor fouling and drift encountered during each deployment period (Wagner et al. 2006; Starkey et al. 2008). The specific conductance data grades less than "excellent" were primarily due to sensor fouling.

Corrections applied to the specific conductance data are listed in Appendix E.

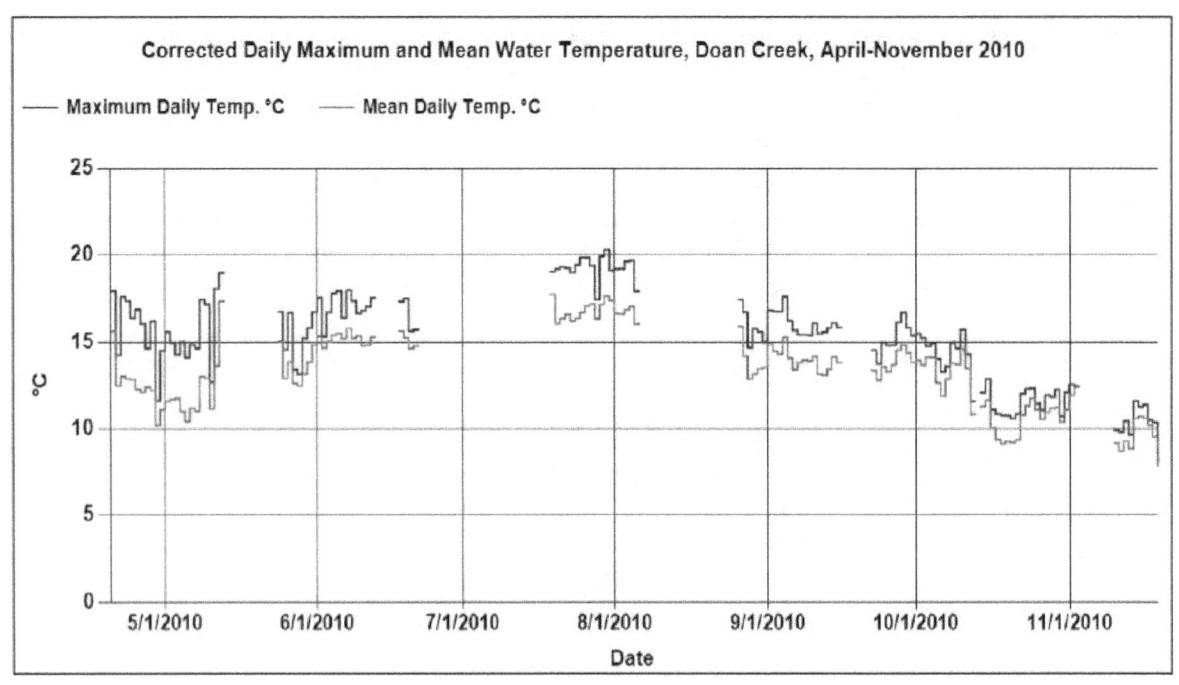

Figure 8. Daily maximum and mean temperature in Doan Creek, WHMI, 2010.

Table 2. Data grade/rating for water temperature each deployment period April-November 2010 Doan Creek, WHMI.

Temperature Data Grade/Rating	From UTC-07:00	To UTC-07:00
EXCELLENT	4/20/2010 14:30	5/14/2010 12:30
EXCELLENT	5/24/2010 16:00	6/12/2010 22:00
FAIR	6/18/2010 17:00	6/21/2010 22:00
GOOD	7/19/2010 15:00	8/5/2010 11:00
GOOD	8/26/2010 15:30	9/15/2010 21:30
GOOD	9/22/2010 16:00	10/12/2010 8:00
EXCELLENT	10/14/2010 16:30	11/2/2010 3:30
GOOD	11/10/2010 19:00	11/19/2010 8:00

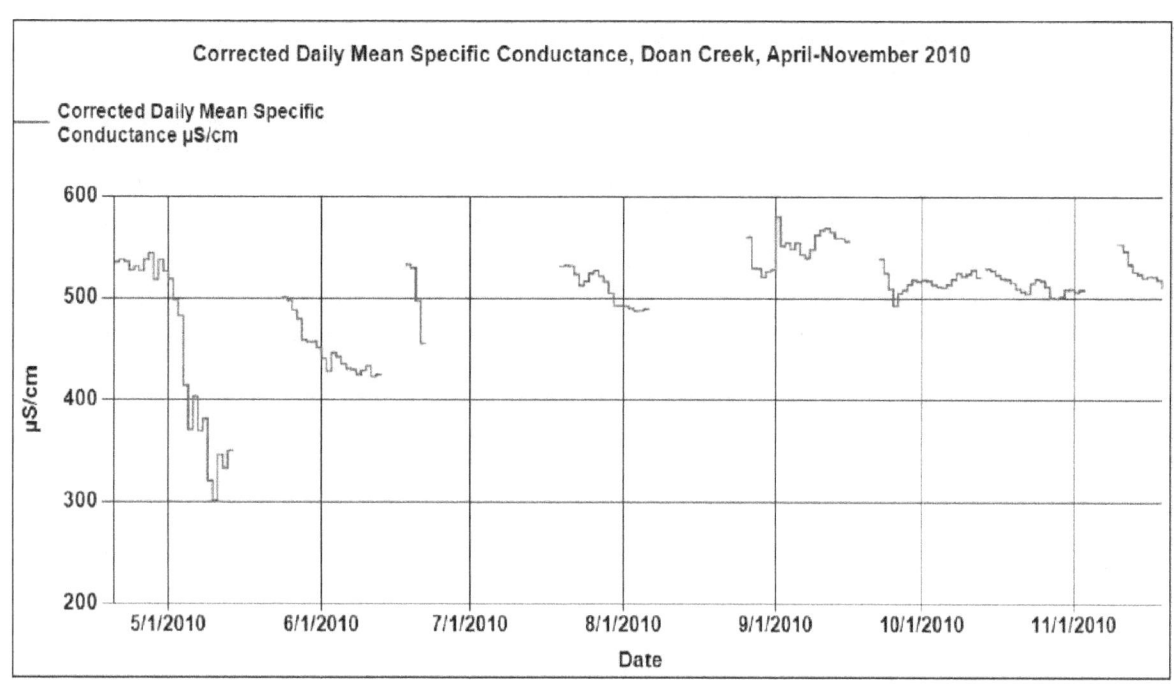

Figure 9. Corrected daily mean specific conductance in Doan Creek, WHMI, 2010.

Table 3. Data grade/rating for specific conductance each deployment period April-November 2010 in Doan Creek, WHMI.

Specific Conductance Data Grade/Rating	From UTC-07:00	To UTC-07:00
EXCELLENT	4/20/2010 14:30	5/14/2010 12:30
EXCELLENT	5/24/2010 16:00	6/12/2010 22:00
FAIR	6/18/2010 17:00	6/21/2010 22:00
EXCELLENT	7/19/2010 15:00	8/5/2010 12:00
GOOD	8/26/2010 15:30	9/22/2010 7:30
FAIR	9/22/2010 16:00	10/14/2010 10:00
GOOD	10/14/2010 16:30	11/2/2010 3:30
EXCELLENT	11/10/2010 19:00	11/19/2010 8:00

- *Dissolved Oxygen:*
  Mean daily minimum dissolved oxygen was 8.6 mg/L and consistently failed to meet (96%) the standards for "class AA" streams (> 9.5 mg/l), but only exceeded "class A" standards (8.0mg/l) during 31% of observations. As expected, minimum dissolved oxygen levels generally corresponded to maximum water temperatures. Figure 10 shows the daily minimum dissolved oxygen and maximum temperatures in Doan Creek from April-November 2010. Table 4 shows the data rating/grade for each deployment period (monthly interval). These standard USGS ratings are based on the degree of sensor fouling and drift encountered during each deployment period (Wagner et al. 2006; Starkey et al. 2008). Data grades of "unusable" were due to heavy fouling and sensor failure. Corrections applied to the dissolved oxygen data are listed in Appendix E.

  Minimum dissolved oxygen levels can likely be increased if water temperatures are reduced via stream shading and increased summer stream flow. However, it is unlikely that class AA standards for dissolved oxygen (> 9.5 mg/l) are attainable when immediately upstream from the park Doan Creek is designated "class A," and has less stringent water quality standards than exist as it flows through the park.

- *pH:*
  The minimum and maximum pH (7.7and 8.5 respectively) were never outside the acceptable regulatory thresholds of 6.5-8.5 pH units and the median (7.9 pH units) was well within this range. Figure 11 shows the daily maximum, minimum, and median pH in Doan Creek from April-November 2010. Table 5 shows the data rating/grade for each deployment period (monthly interval). These standard USGS ratings are based on the degree of sensor fouling and drift encountered during each deployment period (Wagner et al. 2006; Starkey et al. 2008). Data grades of "fair" and "good" were due to a combination of sensor fouling and drift. Corrections applied to the pH data are listed in Appendix E.

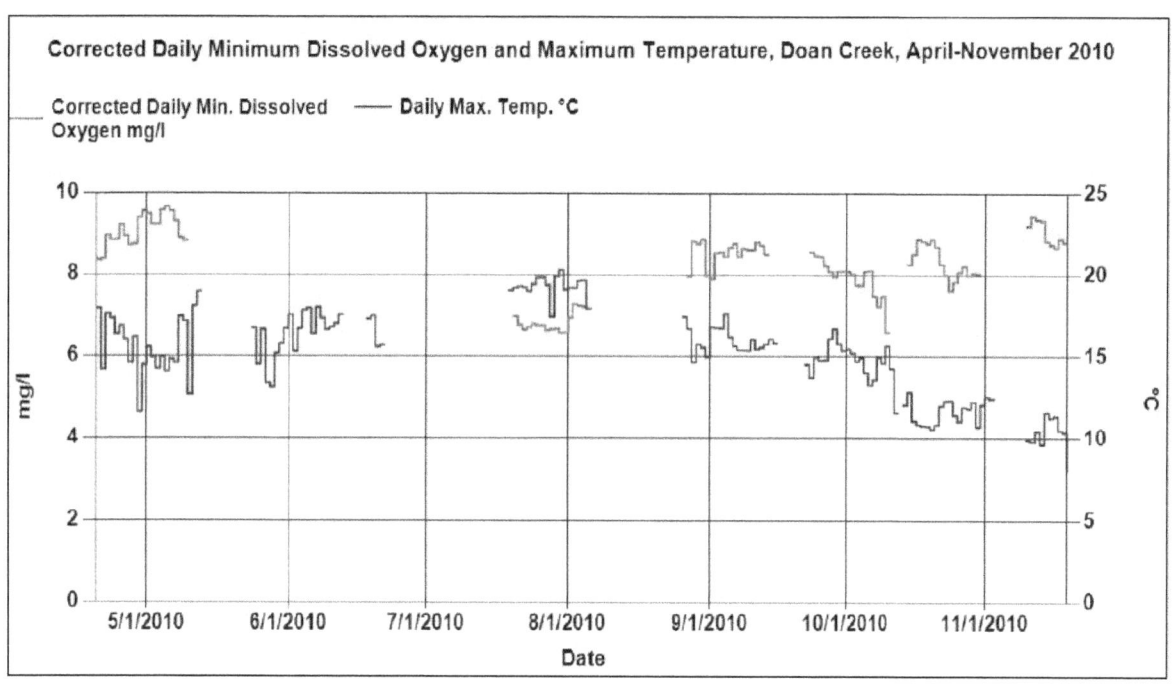

Figure 10. Corrected daily minimum dissolved oxygen and daily maximum temperature in Doan Creek, WHMI, 2010. Note that "unusable" dissolved oxygen data is not displayed in the graph (5/24/2010 to 6/29/2010.

Table 4. Data grade/rating for dissolved oxygen each deployment period April-November 2010 in Doan Creek, WHMI.

Dissolved Oxygen Data Grade/Rating	From UTC-07:00	To UTC-07:00
EXCELLENT	4/20/2010 14:30	5/14/2010 12:30
UNUSEABLE	5/24/2010 16:00	6/10/2010 1:00
UNUSEABLE	6/18/2010 17:00	6/29/2010 9:00
EXCELLENT	7/19/2010 15:00	8/5/2010 11:00
EXCELLENT	8/26/2010 15:30	9/13/2010 20:30
GOOD	9/22/2010 16:00	10/12/2010 6:00
EXCELLENT	10/14/2010 16:30	10/31/2010 1:30
EXCELLENT	11/10/2010 19:00	11/19/2010 8:00

23

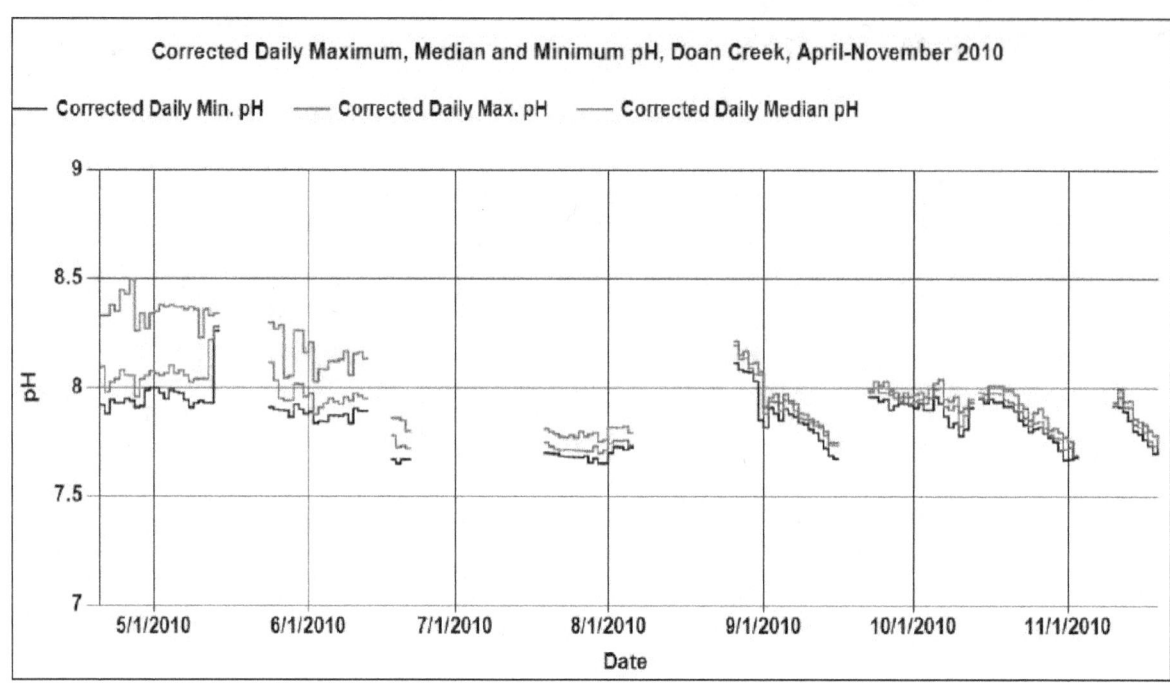

Figure 11. Corrected daily maximum, minimum, and median pH in Doan Creek, WHMI, 2010. Note that the maximum and minimum regulatory thresholds were never exceeded (6.5, 8.5 pH units).

Table 5. Data grade/rating for pH each deployment period April-November2010 in Doan Creek, WHMI.

pH Data Grade/Rating	From UTC-07:00	To UTC-07:00
EXCELLENT	4/20/2010 14:30	5/14/2010 12:30
GOOD	5/24/2010 16:00	6/18/2010 2:00
FAIR	6/18/2010 17:00	6/21/2010 22:00
GOOD	7/19/2010 15:00	8/5/2010 12:00
GOOD	8/26/2010 15:30	9/18/2010 7:07
EXCELLENT	9/22/2010 16:00	10/12/2010 7:00
GOOD	10/14/2010 16:30	11/2/2010 3:30
GOOD	11/10/2010 19:00	11/19/2010 9:00

24

- *Turbidity:*

  Prior to discussion about turbidity in Doan Creek (Figure 12), it should be noted that conclusions based on this data are limited due to poor/unusable data quality (63% of deployments) (Table 6). Sensor fouling due to sediment and sensor drift (possibly associated with the dissolved oxygen sensor failure) were the primary factors influencing data quality. It is important to note that the method detection limit (MDL) for this sensor was 0.3 NTU and the minimum level of quantitation (ML) was 0.90 NTU (Appendix D). Figure 12 shows the corrected daily mean turbidity in the Doan Creek from April-November 2010. Note that data with quality ratings of "unusable" have not been graphed. Corrections that were applied to turbidity data are listed in Appendix E.

  Data indicates that turbidity ranged from <0.3 to 325 NTU. However, due to poor data quality and lack of historic data for this site the UCBN is unable to determine if conditions exceeded the state standard. Regulatory thresholds for turbidity state there should be < 5 NTU increase above background when background NTU < 50, < 10% increase when background NTU > 50. Although conclusions are limited based on the quality of data collected in 2010 it is likely that Doan Creek does experience relatively high levels of turbidity in part due to current upstream land use and recent stream channel restoration/modifications.

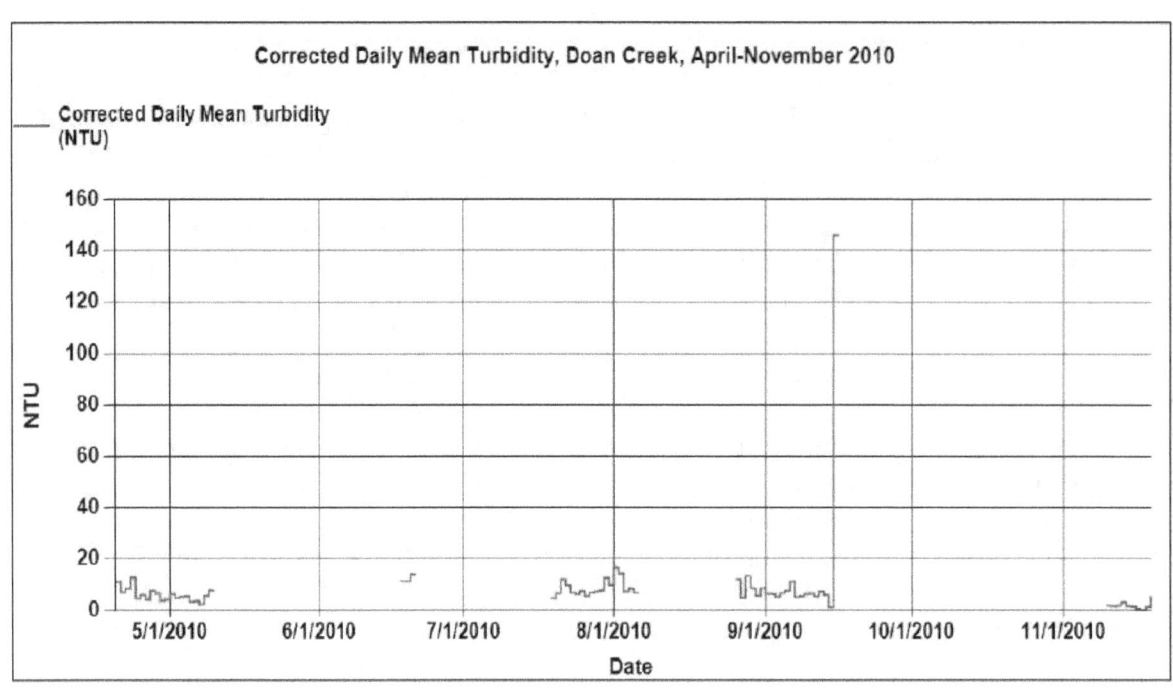

Figure 12. Corrected daily mean turbidity in Doan Creek, WHMI, 2010.Note that the un-usable data grades (blue) presented in table 6 were primarily due to severe fouling, "unusable" dissolved oxygen data is not displayed in the graph (5/24/2010 to 6/10/2010 and 9/22/2010 to 11/2/2010).

Table 6. Data grade/rating for turbidity each deployment period April-November 2010 in Doan Creek, WHMI.

Turbidity Data Grade/Rating	From UTC-07:00	To UTC-07:00
GOOD	4/20/2010 14:30	5/14/2010 12:30
UNUSEABLE	5/24/2010 16:00	6/10/2010 1:00
POOR	6/18/2010 17:00	6/20/2010 19:00
GOOD	7/19/2010 15:00	8/5/2010 12:00
POOR	8/26/2010 15:30	9/15/2010 21:30
UNUSEABLE	9/22/2010 16:00	10/12/2010 6:00
UNUSEABLE	10/14/2010 16:30	11/2/2010 3:30
GOOD	11/10/2010 19:00	11/19/2010 8:00

Macroinvertebrates

Status:

The Hilsenhoff Biotic Index (HBI), which summarizes pollution tolerances of the macroinvertebrate taxa within the sample, indicates that organic pollution in Doan Creek is "unlikely" (HBI= 2.5) (Hilsenhoff 1987, 1988). HBI values generally increase (HBI ranges from 0.0 to 10.0) as nutrient enrichment increases. While HBI is most sensitive to organic pollution, it may also respond to sediment loading, low dissolved oxygen and elevated water temperatures. The US Forest Service (USFS) community tolerance quotient was 96 and indicates that Doan Creek's benthic macroinvertebrate community is impaired. Values of the USFS tolerance quotient range from 20 to just over 100, with lower values indicating better water quality. The very low number of Ephemeroptera, Plecoptera, Trichoptera (EPT) taxa (EPT= 1), lack of long lived taxa (0), and dominance of Oligochaeta in the sample suggests that Doan Creek has impaired habitat, likely due to disturbance and pollution. It is likely that Doan Creek habitat is still recovering from recent channel modifications and, as water quality data indicates, is being severely impacted by elevated water temperatures and low dissolved oxygen levels. As the Doan Creek channel stabilizes we expect to see an increasing number of long-lived taxa and EPT taxa. At the time this report was written, stream channel data from the UCBN's stream channel characteristics monitoring protocol were not available. However, based on past observations, it is likely that lack of suitable cobble/gravel substrate, and homogeneous depths and flows are likely factors of habitat impairment. See Table 7 and Appendix F for additional summary metrics.

It should be noted that typically an observed to expected ratio (OE) is calculated for sites sampled by the PIBO program. However, for Doan Creek the total count of macroinvertebrates fell below the OE model requirements (>200 individuals) and no OE ratio was calculated.

Table 7. Vital sign summary table for benthic macroinvertebrates in Doan Creek, 2011. Note that the entire macroinvertebrate taxa and metrics lists can be found in Appendix F and G.

Doan Creek Macroinvertebrate Summary August 2011	
PIBO Station	**3195**
Sample ID	**147162**
Richness*	8
Shannon's Diversity*	1.57
Simpson's Diversity*	0.74
Evenness*	0.75
# of EPT Taxa*	1
Dominant Family	--
Dominant Taxa	Oligochaeta
Hilsenhoff Biotic Index*	2.5
# of Intolerant Taxa*	1
# of Tolerant Taxa*	1
USFS Community Tolerance Quotient (d)*	96
# of shredder taxa*	1
# of scraper taxa*	0
# of collector-filterer taxa*	0
# of collector-gatherer taxa*	6
# of predator taxa*	1
# of clinger taxa*	0
Long-lived Taxa*	0

Coliform

Status:

The coliform sample from Doan Creek indicated that in early August 2011 *E. coli* levels (110/100 ml) fell below what is considered acceptable in adjacent states (<406/100ml for a single sample). State standards for bacteria are for fecal coliform rather than *E. coli*. (geometric mean of samples <200 cfu/100 ml, <10% of the samples can exceed 400 cfu/100 mL). At the time of sampling, the Walla Walla County health department was unable to run analysis for fecal coliform (Table 8).

Table 8. Results of the coliform sample taken from Doan Creek, August 2011.

Sample Date	Location	Total Coliform	*E. coli*
8/03/2011	Doan Creek– near 2010 water quality monitoring station	>1600/100 ml	110/100 ml

Mill Creek- 2009

Water Chemistry:

Cross Section Survey:
A cross section survey was conducted at the proposed multiprobe deployment location to evaluate if the site was reasonably representative of stream conditions throughout the park. As suggested by the water resource division the UCBN judges overall representativeness primarily on the basis of specific conductance (Starkey et al. 2008).

The 2009 deployment location provided adequate water depth throughout the field season, was easily accessible, and was away from heavily trafficked access points. In addition, the 2009 deployment location was the same as in 2008. Note that in 2009 only a single cross section survey was completed.

A one way analysis of variance (ANOVA) test was conducted to evaluate representativeness (R v2.12.0). Results of the ANOVA showed that there was no significant difference for specific conductance among the transects and the deployment location in June $F(4,44)= 0.434$, $p> 0.05$. In summary, the deployment location was determined to be representative of upstream conditions in June (Figure 13).

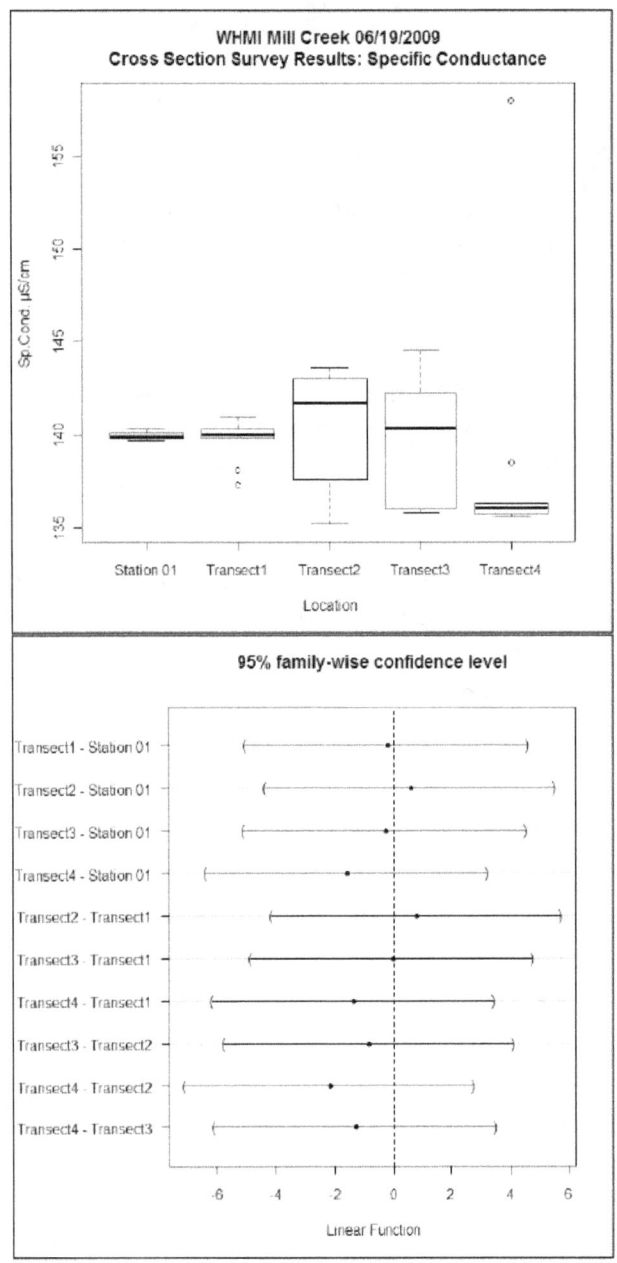

Figure 13. June 2009 cross section survey of Mill Creek, box plot of specific conductance and plot of 95% family-wise confidence level.Note that "Station 01" is the location of multiprobe deployment and the transects progress upstream (1-4).

Status:

Condition of core water quality parameters (2009) along with the corresponding state Department of Ecology (WADOE) regulatory threshold are given in Table 9. For comparison, the condition of core water quality parameters as observed in 2008 are given in Table 10. As in 2008, 2009 data showed that the primary concern in Mill Creek is elevated water temperatures, low dissolved oxygen levels and their effect on native salmonids. In addition, Mill Creek regularly exceeded the upper pH criteria, although with fewer total exceedances than in 2008.

Table 9. Vital sign summary table for water chemistry in Mill Creek June-November, 2009.

Mill Creek Water Chemistry Summary 2009

Measure	Current Condition (June-November, 2009)	State DOE Thresholds [a]	% Exceedance[b]
Temperature (*MDMT, **MDAT)	* MDMT= 26.7 °C ** MDAT= 23.8 °C	***7-DADMax <16 °C	64%
Specific conductance (mean)	232 µS/cm	N/A	N/A
Dissolved oxygen (mean daily min)	7.3 mg/l	>9.5 mg/l Minimum Daily Minimum	78%
pH (mean daily max)	8.4 pH Units	8.5 pH Units, Max (0.5 units human caused variation)	10%
pH (mean daily min)	7.6 pH Units	6.5 pH Units, Min (0.5 units human caused variation)	0%
Turbidity (mean daily max)	4.6 NTU	< 5 NTU increase above background when background NTU < 50, < 10% increase when background NTU > 50	Insufficient data

*MDMT – Maximum Daily Maximum Temperature, **MDAT – Maximum Daily Average Temperature, ***7-DADMax – 7 DayAverage Daily Maximum Temperature, [a] Criteria established for Class AA , [b] Proportion of samples above water quality standard

0-5% exceedance	
5-25% exceedance	
>25% exceedance	

Table 10. Vital sign summary table for water chemistry in Mill Creek June-November, 2008.

Mill Creek Water Chemistry Summary 2008

Measure	Current Condition (June-October, 2008)	State DOE Thresholds [a]	% Exceedance[b]
Temperature (*MDMT, **MDAT)	* MDMT= 25.5°C ** MDAT= 24.0 °C	***7-DADMax <16 °C	80%
Specific conductance (mean)	288 µS/cm	N/A	N/A
Dissolved oxygen (mean daily min)	6.25 mg/l	>9.5 mg/l Minimum Daily Minimum	100%
pH (mean daily max)	8.9 pH Units	8.5 pH Units, Max (0.5 units human caused variation)	23%
pH (mean daily min)	7.6 pH Units	6.5 pH Units, Min (0.5 units human caused variation)	0%
Turbidity (mean daily max)	2.6 NTU	< 5 NTU increase above background when background NTU < 50, < 10% increase when background NTU > 50	Insufficient data

*MDMT – Maximum Daily Maximum Temperature, **MDAT – Maximum Daily Average Temperature, ***7-DADMax – 7 DayAverage Daily Maximum Temperature, [a] Criteria established for Class AA , [b] Proportion of samples above water quality standard.

0-5% exceedance	
5-25% exceedance	
>25% exceedance	

- *Temperature:*
  The maximum daily maximum temperature (MDMT) was 26.7 °C and the maximum daily average temperature (MDAT) was 23.8 °C. Water temperature routinely exceeded (64%) the standard designated for "class AA core summer salmonid habitat" (7-DADMax <16°C), and exceeded the "class B salmonid, spawning, rearing and migration" standard (7-DADMax <17.5°C) during 59% of observations (Baldwin and Stohr 2007). When compared to either "class AA" or "B" standards, these data suggest the need for an increase in base flow and stream shading via riparian vegetation throughout the watershed. In 2009, exceedances of the class AA and class B standards were less than in 2008 (Tables 9 and 10). Despite less frequent exceedance, our data reinforces basin-wide temperature concerns mentioned in the Walla Walla Watershed Temperature TMDL- Water Quality Improvement Report (Baldwin and Stohr 2007), Walla Walla Watershed PCB's, Chlorinated Pesticides....TMDL- Water Quality Implementation Plan (Baldwin et al. 2008) and the 2008 303(d) list (Washington Department of Ecology 2008). Figure 14 shows the daily maximum and mean daily temperatures in Mill Creek from June-November 2009. Table 11 lists the data rating/grade for each deployment period (monthly interval). These standard USGS ratings are based on the degree of sensor fouling and drift encountered during each deployment period (Wagner et al. 2006; Starkey et al. 2008). Data grades less than "excellent" were primarily due to inaccurate field thermometer readings during evaluation of sensor fouling. Corrections that have been applied to the specific conductance data are listed in Appendix E.

  Water temperatures are of particular interest in Mill Creek, given that its designated use include rearing, migration and core summer salmonid habitat; and that it provides habitat for: bull trout (*Salvelinus confluentus*), and steelhead (*Oncorhynchus mykiss*) Implications of elevated water temperatures may include decreased salmonid recruitment, decreased salmonid health, and potential shifts in fish and benthic macroinvertebrate communities (Vannote and Sweeney 1980; McCullough 1999). It is also important to note that elevated water temperatures have the capacity to reduce the total concentration of dissolved oxygen (i.e., there is an inverse relationship between water temperature and dissolved oxygen; Figure 16), thereby impacting aquatic biota.

Maintaining water temperatures suitable for naturally occurring species in Mill Creek will depend on riparian and stream channel conditions basin-wide. For this reason cooperation with other agencies, stakeholders, and adjacent landowners will be critical for improving water temperature.

- *Specific Conductance:*
  Specific conductance ranged from 134.0 to 325.2 μS/cm, with an average specific conductance of 232.0 μS/cm (Figure 15). Table 12 shows the data rating/grade for each deployment period (monthly interval). These standard USGS ratings are based on the degree of sensor fouling and drift encountered during each deployment period (Wagner et al. 2006; Starkey et al. 2008). The specific conductance data grade of "fair" was due to a combination of sensor fouling and drift. Corrections applied to the specific conductance data are listed in Appendix E.

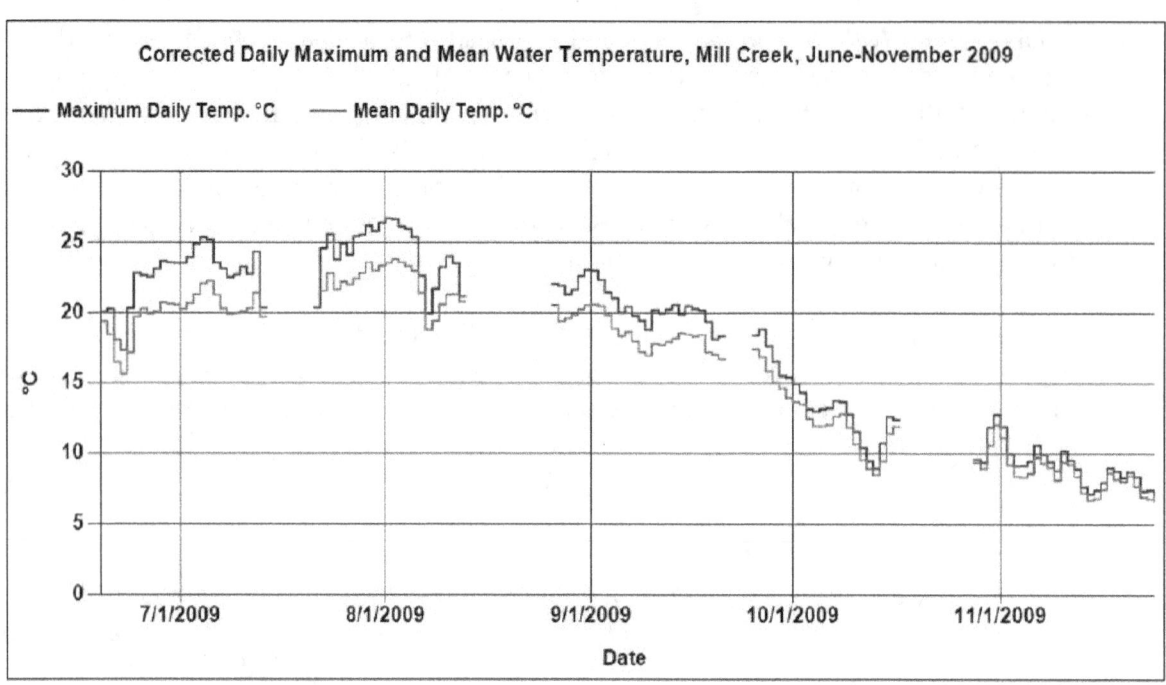

Figure 14. Daily maximum and mean temperature in Mill Creek, WHMI, 2009.

Table 11. Data grade/rating for water temperature each deployment period June-November 2009 in Mill Creek, WHMI.

Temperature Data Grade/Rating	From UTC-07:00	To UTC-07:00
GOOD	6/19/2009 14:45	7/13/2009 4:45
GOOD	7/22/2009 5:00	8/12/2009 4:00
EXCELLENT	8/26/2009 17:30	9/20/2009 21:30
EXCELLENT	9/25/2009 18:00	10/16/2009 11:00
GOOD	10/28/2009 17:00	11/24/2009 11:00

Note that data ratings of "EST Poor" are not shown in the data rating tables. Aquarius time series software versions prior to v2.7 assigned "estimated poor" to the time period between 2 deployments if outliers/erroneous data had been removed (due to low battery power, etc.). "EST Poor" data ratings are maintained in the csv. output from Aquarius, which is stored on the UCBN server.

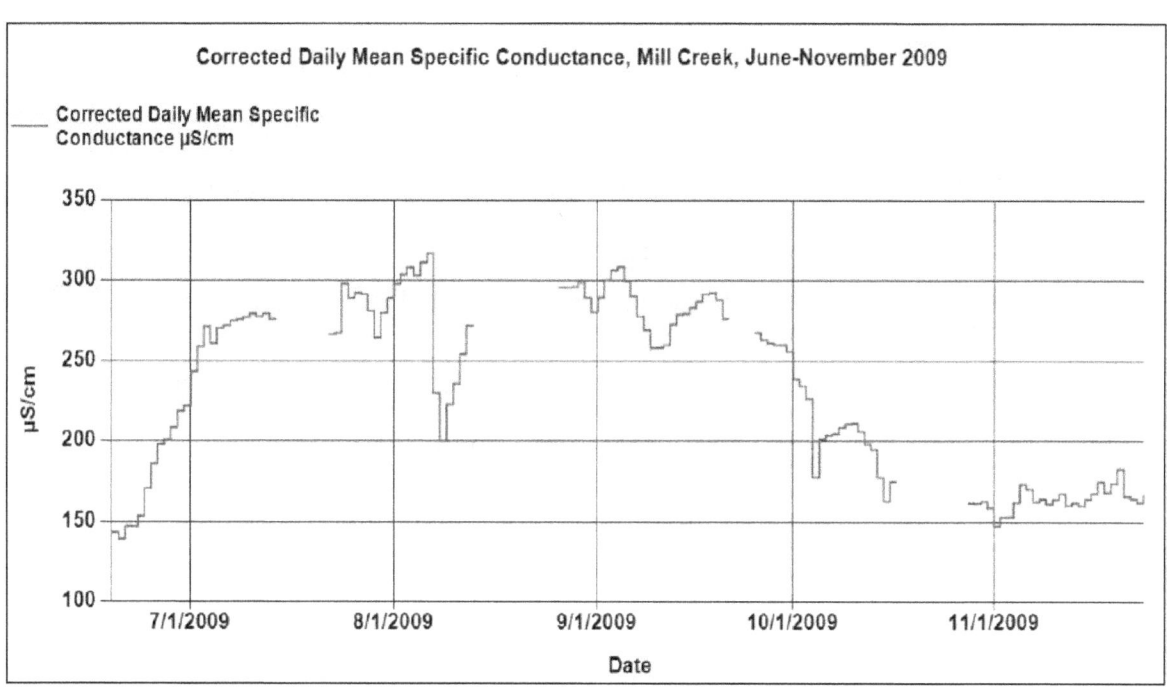

Figure 15. Corrected mean daily specific conductance in Mill Creek, WHMI, 2009.

Table 12. Data grade/rating for specific conductance each deployment period June-November 2009 in Mill Creek, WHMI.

Specific Conductance Data Grade/Rating	From UTC-07:00	To UTC-07:00
EXCELLENT	6/19/2009 14:45	7/13/2009 19:45
EXCELLENT	7/22/2009 5:00	8/12/2009 4:00
EXCELLENT	8/26/2009 17:30	9/20/2009 21:30
EXCELLENT	9/25/2009 18:00	10/16/2009 11:00
FAIR	10/28/2009 17:00	11/24/2009 11:00

- *Dissolved Oxygen:*
  Mean daily minimum dissolved oxygen was 7.3 mg/l and the minimum daily minimum fell below the regulatory threshold for "class AA" streams (>9.5 mg/l min. daily min.) during 78% of observations. In addition, dissolved oxygen fell below the "class B special condition" standard for Mill Creek (> 5.0 mg/l) during 12% of observations. In 2009, exceedances of the class AA and class B special condition standards were less frequent than in 2008 (Table 9). In Mill Creek, low dissolved oxygen levels are likely driven by two sources; elevated temperatures and eutrophication from upstream sources. If water temperatures fell below regulatory thresholds it is likely that dissolved oxygen levels in the lower portion of Mill Creek would meet the special condition standard of >5.0 mg/l and reduce exceedances of the "class AA" standard (>9.5 mg/l). However, it is unlikely that class AA standards for dissolved oxygen (> 9.5 mg/l) are attainable when immediately upstream/downstream from the park Mill Creek is designated "class B special condition" (> 5.0 mg/l) and has less stringent water quality standards than exist as it flows through the park.

  Figure 16 shows the daily minimum dissolved oxygen and maximum temperatures in Mill Creek from June-November 2009. Table 13 shows the data rating/grade for each deployment period (monthly interval). These standard USGS ratings are based on the degree of sensor fouling and drift encountered during each deployment period (Wagner et al. 2006; Starkey et al. 2008). The data grades less than "excellent" were due to a combination of calibration drift and sensor fouling. Corrections applied to the dissolved oxygen data are listed in Appendix E.

- *pH:*
  The minimum and maximum pH was 7.16 and 9.12 pH units respectively. pH exceeded the upper threshold of 8.5 pH units in 10% of observations. It should be noted that in 2008, pH exceeded the upper pH criteria (8.5 pH units) in 23% of observations. No observations fell below the lower pH threshold (6.5 pH units). Figure 17 shows the daily maximum, minimum, and median pH in Mill Creek from June-November 2009. Table 14 shows the data rating/grade for each deployment period (monthly interval). These standard USGS ratings are based on the degree of sensor fouling and drift encountered during each deployment period (Wagner et al. 2006; Starkey et al. 2008). The data grade of "good" was primarily due to sensor fouling and to a lesser extent sensor drift. Corrections applied to the pH data are listed in Appendix E.

  Elevated pH may be cause for concern as it may indicate pollution from an upstream source. Monitoring of pH in 2014 will help establish if there is a trend for pH levels in Mill Creek.

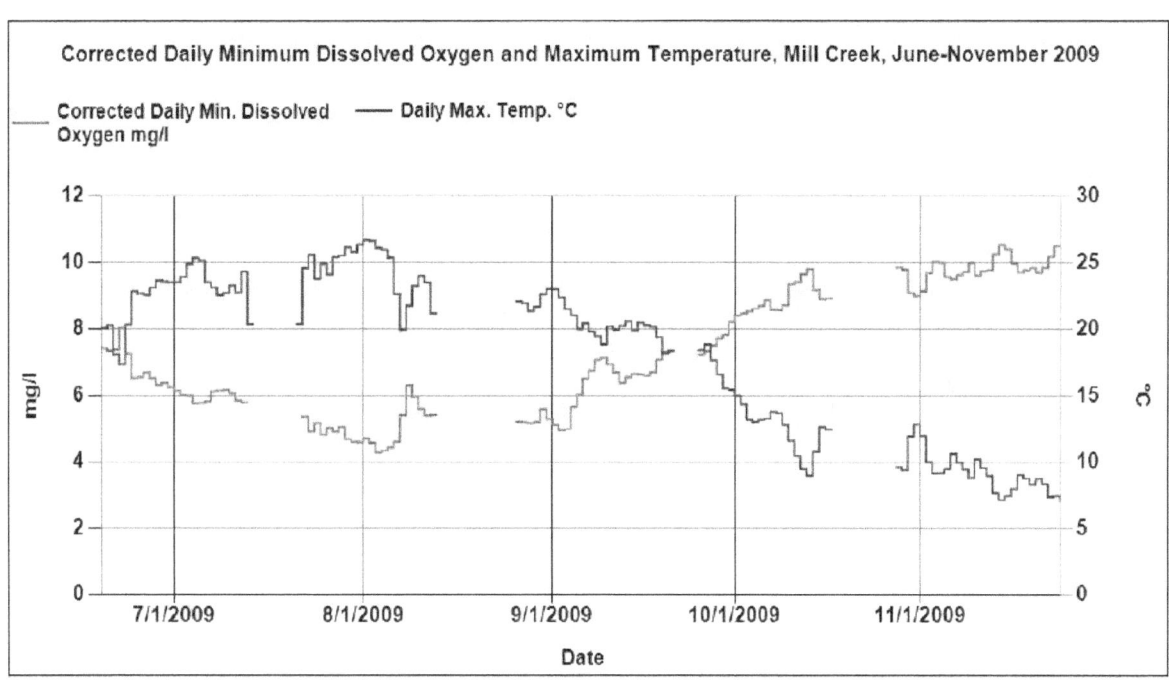

Figure 16. Corrected daily minimum dissolved oxygen and daily maximum temperature in Mill Creek, WHMI, 2009.

Table 13. Data grade/rating for dissolved oxygen each deployment period June-November 2009 in Mill Creek, WHMI.

Dissolved Oxygen Data Grade/Rating	From UTC-07:00	To UTC-07:00
EXCELLENT	6/19/2009 14:45	7/12/2009 17:45
FAIR	7/22/2009 5:00	8/12/2009 4:00
GOOD	8/26/2009 17:30	9/19/2009 20:30
EXCELLENT	9/25/2009 18:00	10/16/2009 11:00
EXCELLENT	10/28/2009 17:00	11/24/2009 0:00

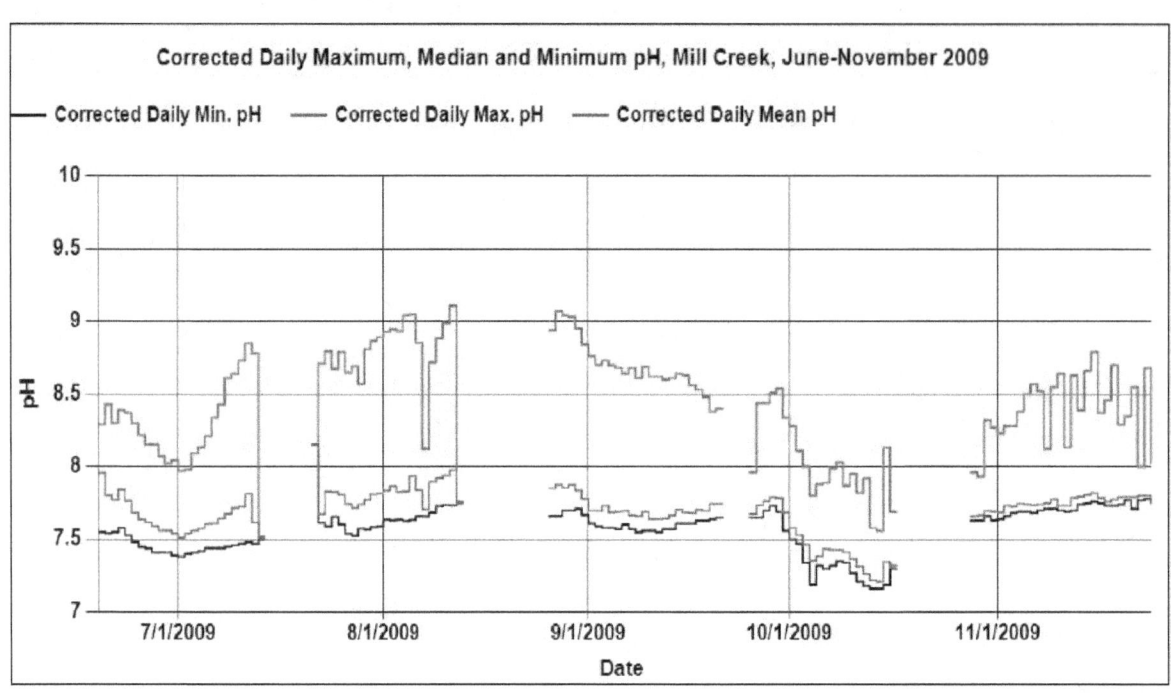

Figure 17. Corrected daily maximum, minimum, and median pH in Mill Creek, WHMI, 2009.

Table 14. Data grade/rating for pH each deployment period June-November 2009 in Mill Creek, WHMI.

pH Data Grade/Rating	From UTC-07:00	To UTC-07:00
EXCELLENT	6/19/2009 14:45	7/13/2009 4:45
GOOD	7/22/2009 5:00	8/12/2009 4:00
EXCELLENT	8/26/2009 17:30	9/20/2009 21:30
EXCELLENT	9/25/2009 18:00	10/16/2009 11:00
EXCELLENT	10/28/2009 17:00	11/24/2009 11:00

- *Turbidity:*
  Mean daily maximum turbidity in Mill Creek between June and November 2009 was 4.6 NTU and turbidity ranged from <0.1 to 84.7 NTU. The regulatory threshold for turbidity states that the following are acceptable turbidity levels, "< 5 NTU increase above background when background NTU < 50, < 10% increase when background NTU > 50." Given that 2009 represents the second year of monitoring and that background levels are important in the determination of percent exceedance, no exceedance was calculated for this parameter. Following multiple years of monitoring in Mill Creek, the UCBN may set a background level for Mill Creek as it flows through WHMI. It is important to note that the method detection limit (MDL) for this sensor was 0.1 NTU and the minimum level of quantitation (ML) was 0.38 NTU (Appendix D).

38

Figure 18 shows the daily mean turbidity in Mill Creek from June-November 2009. Table 15 shows the data rating/grade for each deployment period (monthly interval). These standard USGS ratings are based on the degree of sensor fouling and drift encountered during each deployment period (Wagner et al. 2006; Starkey et al. 2008). The data grades less than "excellent" were due to a combination of calibration drift and sensor fouling. Corrections applied to turbidity data are listed in Appendix E.

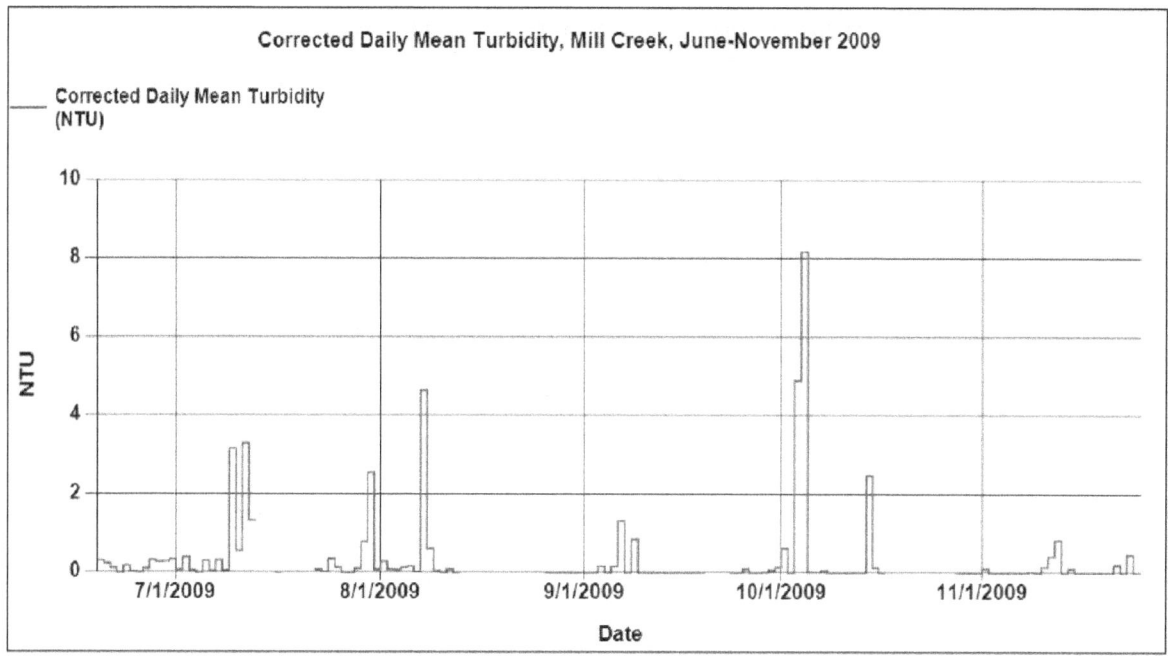

Figure 18. Corrected daily mean turbidity in Mill Creek, WHMI, 2009.

Table 15. Data grade/rating for turbidity each deployment period June-November 2009 Mill Creek, WHMI.

Turbidity Data Grade/Rating	From UTC-07:00	To UTC-07:00
GOOD	6/19/2009 14:45	7/13/2009 2:45
EXCELLENT	7/22/2009 5:00	8/12/2009 4:00
FAIR	8/26/2009 17:30	9/18/2009 20:30
FAIR	9/25/2009 18:00	10/16/2009 11:00
FAIR	10/28/2009 17:00	11/24/2009 11:00

Macroinvertebrates

Status:
No macroinvertebrate samples were taken from Mill Creek in 2009. See the Mill Creek 2011 results section for recent macroinvertebrate results or Starkey 2009 for results of monitoring that occurred in 2008.

Coliform

Status:
No Coliform or *E. coli* samples were drawn from Mill Creek in 2009. See Mill Creek 2011 results section for recent sample results.

Mill Creek- 2011

Water Chemistry:

Cross Section Survey:
A cross section survey was conducted at the proposed multiprobe deployment location to evaluate if the site was reasonably representative of stream conditions throughout the park. As suggested by the water resource division the UCBN judges overall representativeness primarily on the basis of specific conductance (Starkey et al. 2008).

The 2011 deployment location provided adequate water depth throughout the field season, was easily accessible, and was away from heavily trafficked access points. In addition, the 2011 deployment location was the same as in 2008 and 2009.

A one way analysis of variance (ANOVA) test was conducted to evaluate representativeness (R v2.12.0). Results of the ANOVA showed that there was no significant difference for specific conductance among the transects and the deployment location in June $F(4,44)=1.42$, $p > 0.05$ and a significant difference in November $F(4,43)= 17.8$, $p < 0.05$.

To determine where the difference in representativeness occurred, a post hoc Tukey's test was conducted (R v2.12.0). Relative to specific conductance, results of the Tukey's test for the cross section conducted in November indicates that the deployment location was significantly different from transect 4 (Figure 20).

In summary, the deployment location was shown to be representative when monitoring began in June (Figure 19). The November cross section survey indicated the monitoring station may not have been representative of conditions near transect 4; however, this may have been largely due to the fact that transect 4 fell near the confluence of Doan Creek with Mill Creek. As such, water from Doan Creek may not have fully mixed until farther downstream (i.e. transect 3). This monitoring location is still considered the most suitable location for permanent deployment.

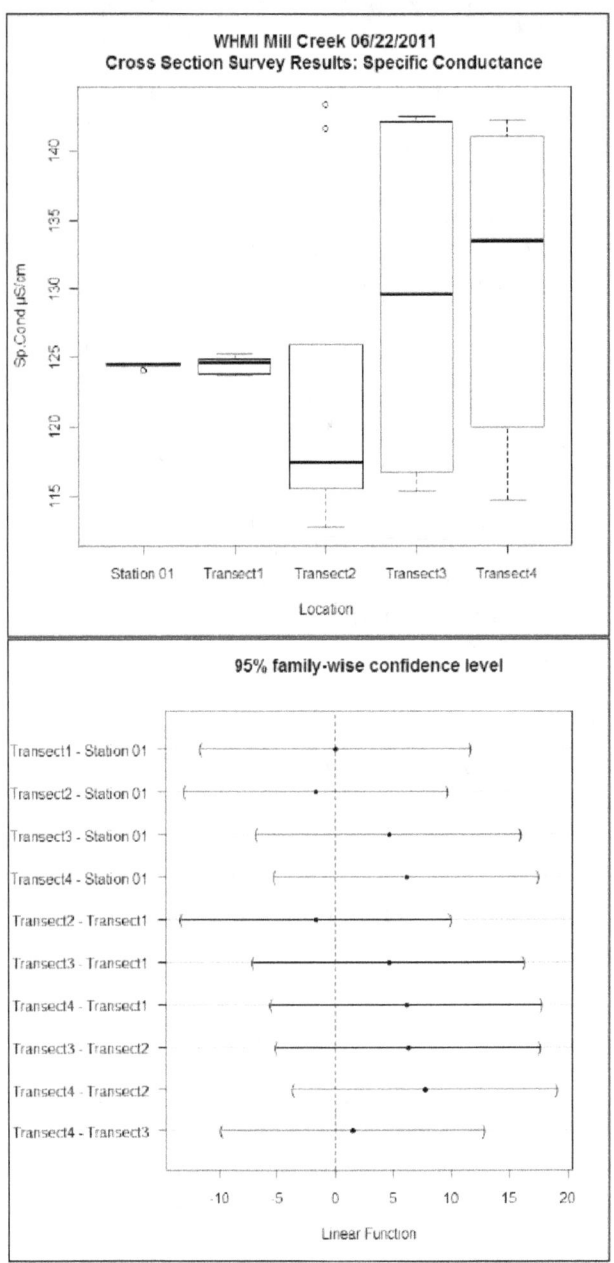

Figure 19. June 2011 cross section survey of Mill Creek, box plot of specific conductance and plot of 95% family-wise confidence level.Note that "Station 01" is the location of multiprobe deployment and the transects progress upstream (1-4).

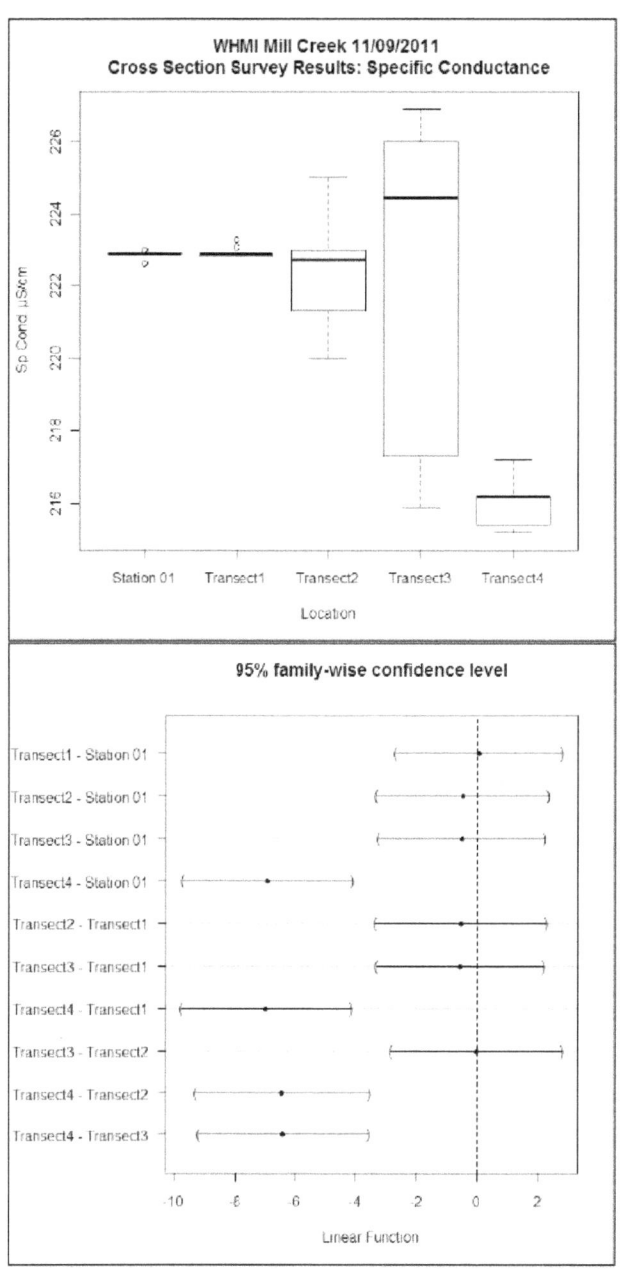

Figure 20. November 2011 cross section survey of Mill Creek, box plot of specific conductance and plot of 95% family-wise confidence level.Note that "Station 01" is the location of multiprobe deployment and the transects progress upstream (1-4)

Status:

Condition of core water quality parameters (2011) along with the corresponding state Department of Ecology (WADOE) regulatory threshold are given in Table 16. For comparison, the condition of core water quality parameters as observed in 2009 are given in Table 17. For a summary of water quality conditions in 2008 refer to Table 10 and Starkey 2009. As in 2008 and 2009, the 2011 data showed that the primary concerns in Mill Creek are elevated water temperatures, low dissolved oxygen levels and their effect on native salmonids. In addition, Mill Creek regularly exceeded the upper pH criteria, although with fewer total exceedances than in 2008, but more than in 2009.

Table 16. Vital sign summary table for water chemistry in Mill Creek June-November, 2011.

Mill Creek Water Chemistry Summary 2011

Measure	Current Condition (June-November, 2011)	State DOE Thresholds [a]	% Exceedance [b]
Temperature (*MDMT, **MDAT)	* MDMT= 24.5 °C ** MDAT= 21.7 °C	***7-DADMax <16 °C	72%
Specific conductance (mean)	278.7 µS/cm	N/A	N/A
Dissolved oxygen (mean daily min)	7.1 mg/l	>9.5 mg/l Minimum Daily Minimum	100%
pH (mean daily max)	8.7 pH Units	8.5 pH Units, Max (0.5 units human caused variation)	19%
pH (mean daily min)	7.6 pH Units	6.5 pH Units, Min (0.5 units human caused variation)	0%
Turbidity (mean daily max)	Insufficient data due to poor data quality	< 5 NTU increase above background when background NTU < 50, < 10% increase when background NTU > 50	Insufficient data
E. coli	130 cfu/100 ml	No state standard for E. coli. In adjacent states, individual samples <406/100ml are generally considered acceptable	0%

*MDMT – Maximum Daily Maximum Temperature, **MDAT – Maximum Daily Average Temperature, ***7-DADMax – 7 DayAverage Daily Maximum Temperature, [a] Criteria established for Class AA , [b] Proportion of samples above water quality standard

0-5% exceedance	
5-25% exceedance	
>25% exceedance	

Table 17. Vital sign summary table for water chemistry in Mill Creek June-November, 2009.

Mill Creek Water Chemistry Summary 2009

Measure	Current Condition (June-November, 2009)	State DOE Thresholds [a]	% Exceedance[b]
Temperature (*MDMT, **MDAT)	* MDMT= 26.7 °C ** MDAT= 23.8 °C	***7-DADMax <16 °C	64%
Specific conductance (mean)	232 µS/cm	N/A	N/A
Dissolved oxygen (mean daily min)	7.3 mg/l	>9.5 mg/l Minimum Daily Minimum	78%
pH (mean daily max)	8.4 pH Units	8.5 pH Units, Max (0.5 units human caused variation)	10%
pH (mean daily min)	7.6 pH Units	6.5 pH Units, Min (0.5 units human caused variation)	0%
Turbidity (mean daily max)	4.6 NTU	< 5 NTU increase above background when background NTU < 50, < 10% increase when background NTU > 50	Insufficient data

*MDMT – Maximum Daily Maximum Temperature, **MDAT – Maximum Daily Average Temperature, ***7-DADMax – 7 DayAverage Daily Maximum Temperature, [a] Criteria established for Class AA , [b] Proportion of samples above water quality standard

0-5% exceedance	
5-25% exceedance	
>25% exceedance	

- *Temperature:*

  The maximum daily maximum temperature (MDMT) was 24.5 °C and the maximum daily average temperature (MDAT) was 21.7 °C. Water temperature routinely exceeded (72%) the standard designated for "class AA core summer salmonid habitat" (7-DADMax <16°C), and exceeded the "class B salmonid, spawning, rearing and migration" standard (7-DADMax <17.5°C) during 67% of observations (Baldwin and Stohr 2007). When compared to either "class AA" or "B" standards, these data suggest the need for an increase in base flow and stream shading via riparian vegetation throughout the watershed. In 2011, exceedances of the class AA and class B standards were less than in 2008; however, in 2011 exceedances were more frequent than in 2009 (Tables 10, 16 and 17). Data from 2011 reinforces previous UCBN findings (Starkey 2009) and basin-wide temperature concerns mentioned in the Walla Walla Watershed Temperature TMDL- Water Quality Improvement Report (Baldwin and Stohr 2007), Walla Walla Watershed PCB's, Chlorinated Pesticides....TMDL- Water Quality Implementation Plan (Baldwin et al. 2008) and the 2008 303(d) list (Washington Department of Ecology 2008). Figure 21 shows the daily maximum and mean daily temperatures in Mill Creek from June-November 2011. Table 18 lists the data rating/grade for each deployment period (monthly interval). These standard USGS ratings are based on the degree of sensor fouling and drift encountered during each deployment period (Wagner et al. 2006; Starkey et al. 2008). Data grades less than "excellent" were primarily due to inaccurate field thermometer readings during evaluation of sensor fouling. Corrections that have been applied to the specific conductance data are listed in Appendix E.

As mentioned in the previous results section (Mill Creek- 2009), water temperatures are of particular interest in Mill Creek, given that its designated use include rearing, migration and core summer salmonid habitat; and that it provides habitat for: bull trout (*Salvelinus confluentus*), and steelhead (*Oncorhynchus mykiss*) Implications of elevated water temperatures may include decreased salmonid recruitment, decreased salmonid health, and potential shifts in fish and benthic macroinvertebrate communities (Vannote and Sweeney 1980; McCullough 1999). It is also important to note that elevated water temperatures have the capacity to reduce the total concentration of dissolved oxygen (i.e., there is an inverse relationship between water temperature and dissolved oxygen; Figure 23), thereby impacting aquatic biota.

Maintaining water temperatures suitable for naturally occurring species in Mill Creek will depend on riparian and stream channel conditions basin-wide. For this reason cooperation with other agencies, stakeholders, and adjacent landowners will be critical for improving water temperature.

- *Specific Conductance:*
  Specific conductance ranged from 121.0 to 342.0 μS/cm, with an average specific conductance of 278.7 μS/cm (Figure 22). Table 19 shows the data rating/grade for each deployment period (monthly interval). These standard USGS ratings are based on the degree of sensor fouling and drift encountered during each deployment period (Wagner et al. 2006; Starkey et al. 2008). The specific conductance data grades of "good" were due primarily to sensor fouling. Corrections applied to the specific conductance data are listed in Appendix E.

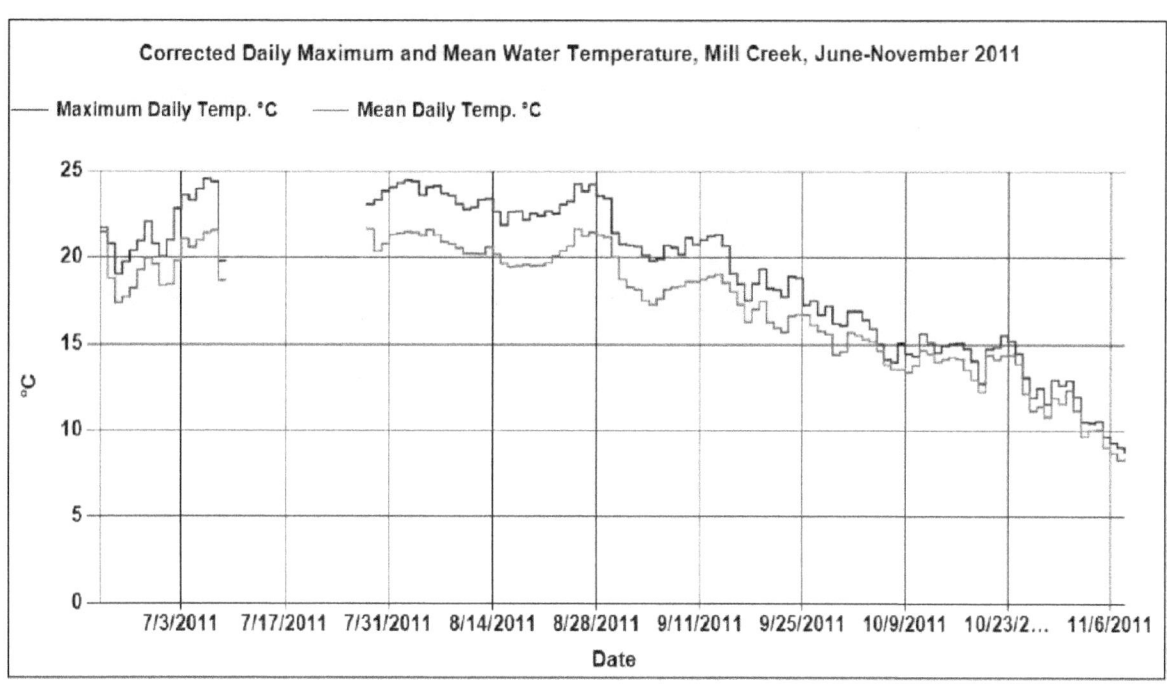

Figure 21. Daily maximum and mean temperature in Mill Creek, WHMI, 2011.

Table 18. Data grade/rating for water temperature each deployment period June-November 2011 in Mill Creek, WHMI.

Temperature Data Grade/Rating	From UTC-07:00	To UTC-07:00
GOOD	6/22/2011 16:00	7/8/2011 9:00
GOOD	7/28/2011 15:15	8/24/2011 8:15
FAIR	8/24/2011 16:00	9/22/2011 11:00
EXCELLENT	9/22/2011 16:30	10/19/2011 11:30
GOOD	10/20/2011 13:30	11/8/2011 9:30

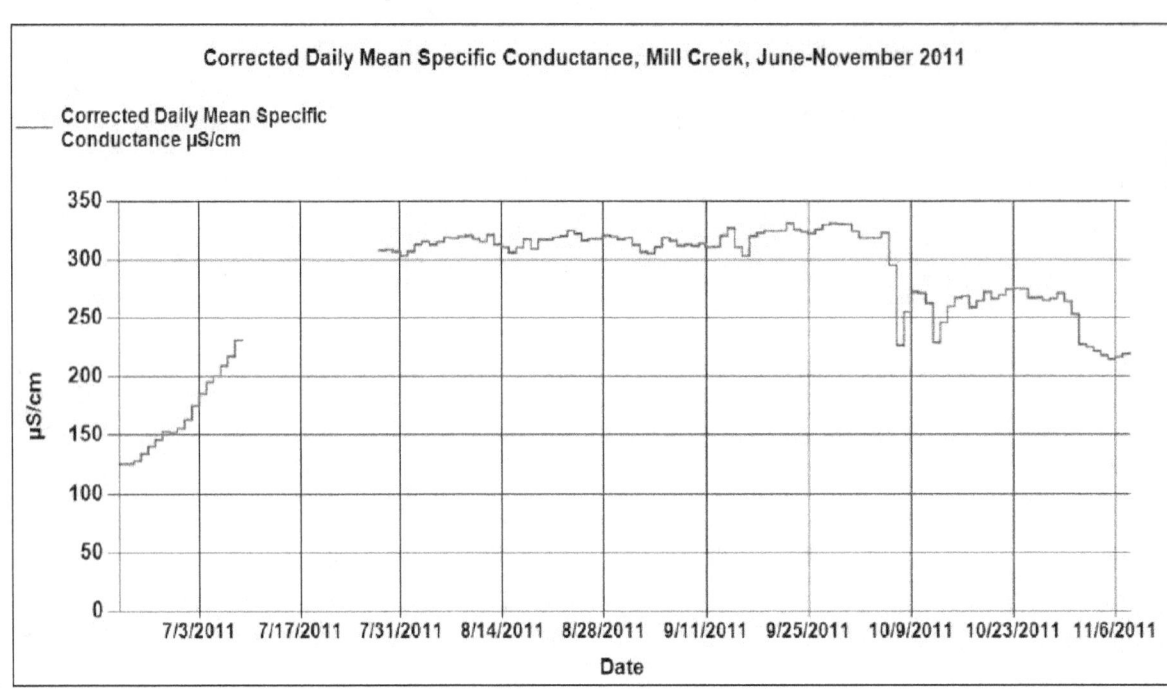

Figure 22. Corrected mean daily specific conductance in Mill Creek, WHMI, 2011.

Table 19. Data grade/rating for specific conductance each deployment period June-November 2011 in Mill Creek, WHMI.

Specific Conductance Data Grade/Rating	From UTC-07:00	To UTC-07:00
EXCELLENT	6/22/2011 16:00	7/8/2011 9:00
GOOD	7/28/2011 15:15	8/24/2011 8:15
GOOD	8/24/2011 16:00	9/22/2011 11:00
GOOD	9/22/2011 16:30	10/19/2011 11:30
EXCELLENT	10/20/2011 13:30	11/8/2011 9:30

- *Dissolved Oxygen:*
  Mean daily minimum dissolved oxygen was 7.1 mg/l and the minimum daily minimum fell below the regulatory threshold for "class AA" streams (>9.5 mg/l min. daily min.) during 100% of observations. In addition, dissolved oxygen fell below the "class B special condition" standard for Mill Creek (> 5.0 mg/l) during 2% of observations. In 2011, exceedances of the class AA standard were with the same frequency as in 2008 and more frequent than in 2009. Class B special condition standard exceedances were less frequent than in 2008 but more frequent than in 2009. As mentioned in the previous results section (Mill Creek- 2009), low dissolved oxygen levels are likely driven by two sources; elevated temperatures and eutrophication from upstream sources. If water temperatures fell below regulatory thresholds it is likely that dissolved oxygen levels in the lower portion of Mill Creek would meet the special condition standard of >5.0 mg/l and reduce exceedances of the "class AA" standard (>9.5 mg/l). However, it is unlikely that class AA standards for dissolved oxygen (> 9.5 mg/l) are attainable when immediately upstream/downstream from the park Mill Creek is designated "class B special condition" (> 5.0 mg/l) and has less stringent water quality standards than exist as it flows through the park.

  Figure 23 shows the daily minimum dissolved oxygen and maximum temperatures in Mill Creek from June-November 2011. Table 20 shows the data rating/grade for each deployment period (monthly interval). These standard USGS ratings are based on the degree of sensor fouling and drift encountered during each deployment period (Wagner et al. 2006; Starkey et al. 2008). The data grade of "poor" was primarily due to sensor fouling and the data grade of "unverified" was due to sensor failure during the deployment period (i.e. could not evaluate sensor drift or fouling during site visit). Corrections applied to the dissolved oxygen data are listed in Appendix E.

- *pH:*
  The minimum and maximum pH was 7.46 and 9.09 pH units respectively. pH exceeded the upper threshold of 8.5 pH units in 19% of observations. It should be noted that in 2008, pH exceeded the upper pH criteria (8.5 pH units) in 23% of observations and in 2009 during 10% of observations. No observations fell below the lower pH threshold (6.5 pH units). Figure 24 shows the daily maximum, minimum, and median pH in Mill Creek from June-November 2011. Table 21 shows the data rating/grade for each deployment period (monthly interval). These standard USGS ratings are based on the degree of sensor fouling and drift encountered during each deployment period (Wagner et al. 2006; Starkey et al. 2008). The data grade of "good" was due to a combination of sensor fouling and sensor drift. Corrections applied to the pH data are listed in Appendix E.

  Elevated pH may be cause for concern as it may indicate pollution from an upstream source. Monitoring of pH in 2014 will help establish if there is a trend for pH levels in Mill Creek.

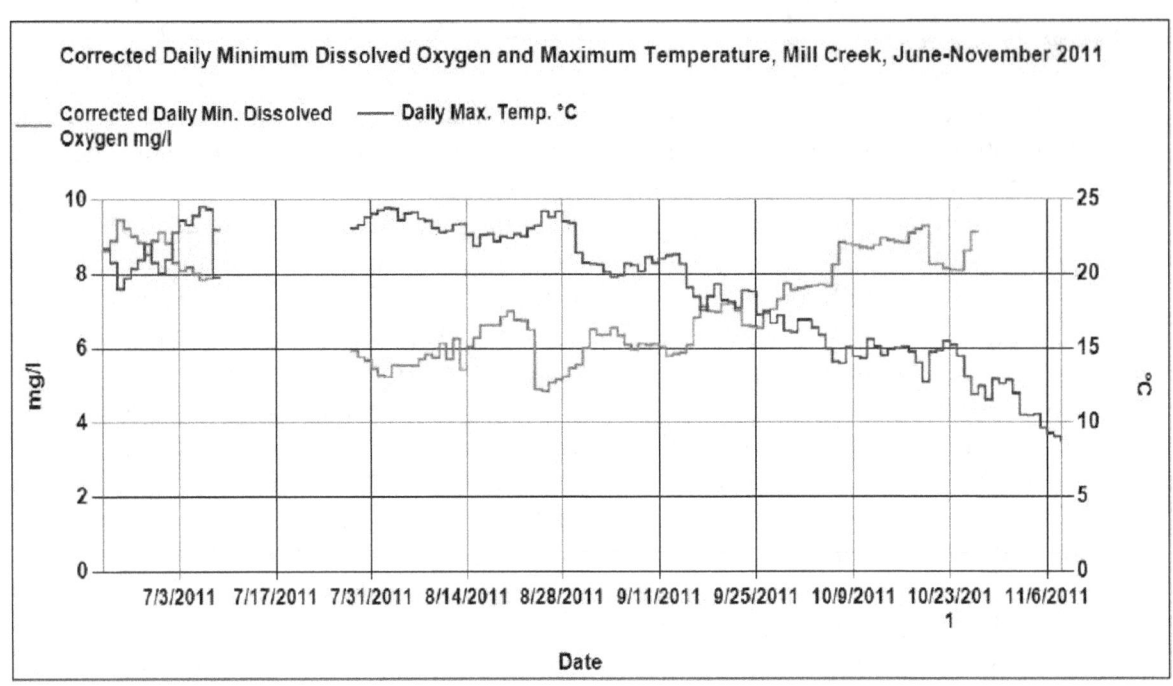

Figure 23. Corrected daily minimum dissolved oxygen and daily maximum temperature in Mill Creek, WHMI, 2011.

Table 20. Data grade/rating for dissolved oxygen each deployment period June-November 2011 in Mill Creek, WHMI.

Dissolved Oxygen Data Grade/Rating	From UTC-07:00	To UTC-07:00
FAIR	6/22/2011 16:00	7/8/2011 9:00
POOR	7/28/2011 15:15	8/24/2011 8:15
GOOD	8/24/2011 16:00	9/22/2011 11:00
FAIR	9/22/2011 16:30	10/19/2011 11:30
UNVERIFIED	10/20/2011 13:30	11/8/2011 9:30

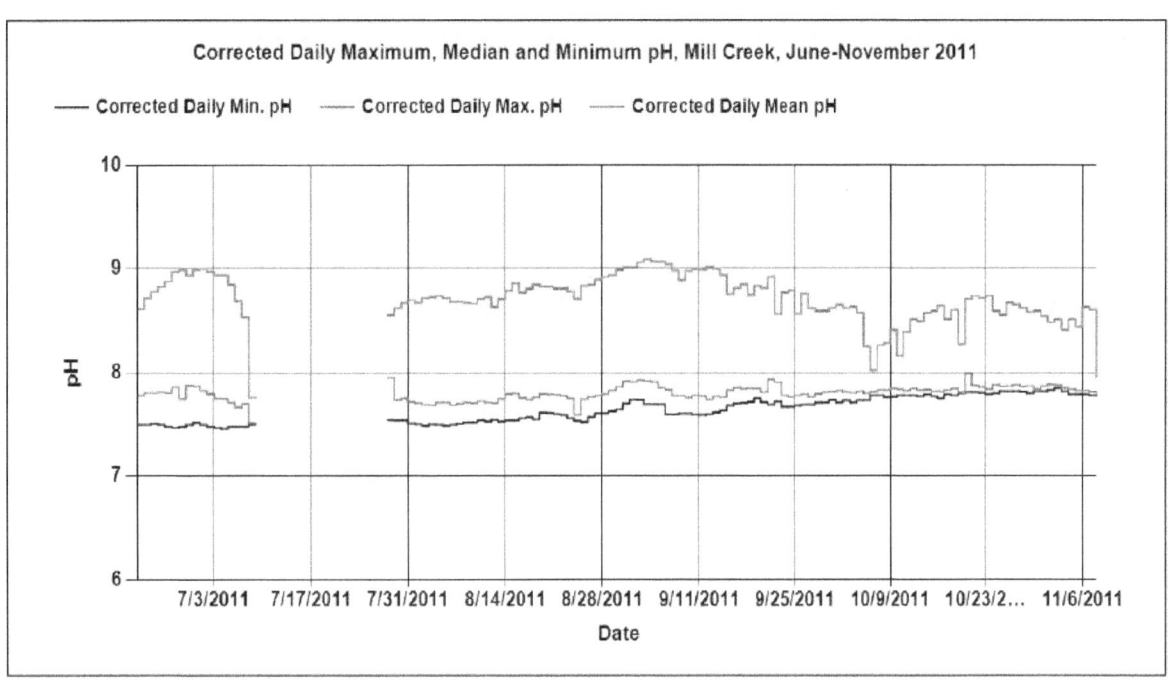

Figure 24. Corrected daily maximum, minimum, and median pH in Mill Creek, WHMI, 2011.

Table 21. Data grade/rating for pH each deployment period June-November 2011 in Mill Creek, WHMI.

pH Data Grade/Rating	From UTC-07:00	To UTC-07:00
EXCELLENT	6/22/2011 16:00	7/8/2011 9:00
EXCELLENT	7/28/2011 15:15	8/24/2011 8:15
GOOD	8/24/2011 16:00	9/22/2011 11:00
EXCELLENT	9/22/2011 16:30	10/19/2011 11:30
EXCELLENT	10/20/2011 13:30	11/8/2011 9:30

- *Turbidity:*
  Prior to discussion about turbidity in Mill Creek in 2011 (Figure 25), it should be noted that conclusions based on this data are limited due to very poor/unusable data quality (Table 22). Sensor fouling due to sediment, sensor drift (possibly associated with the dissolved oxygen sensor failure) and turbidity sensor failure all negatively influenced data quality. It is important to note that the method detection limit (MDL) for this sensor was 0.6 NTU and the minimum level of quantitation (ML) was 1.86 NTU (Appendix D). Figure 25 shows the raw (uncorrected) daily mean turbidity in the Mill Creek from June-November 2011. Raw values were graphed because the program used to manage the water quality data (AQUAIRUS) will only graph corrected data if it has a data grade better than "unusable" (i.e. Poor–Excellent). Note that the data grade of "unverified" was due to sensor failure during the deployment period (i.e. could not evaluate sensor drift or fouling during site visit). Corrections applied to turbidity data are listed in Appendix E.

Corrected data indicates that turbidity ranged from <0.6 to 14.4 NTU. However, due to poor data quality and lack of historic data for this site the UCBN is unable to determine if conditions exceeded the state standard. Regulatory thresholds for turbidity state there should be < 5 NTU increase above background when background NTU < 50, < 10% increase when background NTU > 50.

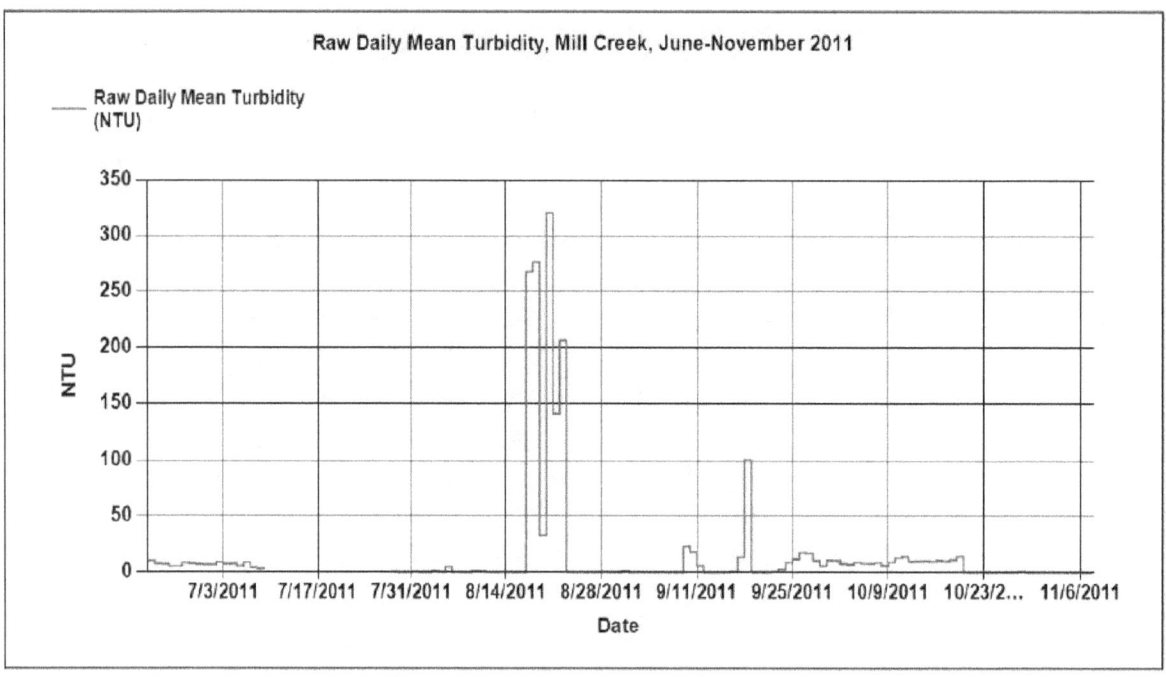

Figure 25. Corrected daily mean turbidity in Mill Creek, WHMI, 2011.

Table 22. Data grade/rating for turbidity each deployment period June-November 2011 Mill Creek, WHMI.

Turbidity Data Grade/Rating	From UTC-07:00	To UTC-07:00
UNUSEABLE	6/22/2011 16:00	7/8/2011 9:00
UNUSABLE	7/28/2011 15:15	8/24/2011 8:15
UNUSABLE	8/24/2011 16:00	9/22/2011 11:00
UNUSABLE	9/22/2011 16:30	10/19/2011 11:30
UNVERIFIED	10/20/2011 13:30	11/8/2011 9:30

Macroinvertebrates

Status:

The Hilsenhoff Biotic Index (HBI), which summarizes pollution tolerances of the macroinvertebrate taxa within the sample, indicates that Mill Creek has "possible slight organic pollution" (HBI= 4.16) (Hilsenhoff 1987, 1988). HBI values generally increase (HBI ranges from 0.0 to 10.0) as nutrient enrichment increases. While HBI is most sensitive to organic pollution, it may also respond to sediment loading, low dissolved oxygen and elevated water temperatures. The US Forest Service (USFS) community tolerance quotient was 88 and indicates that Mill Creek's benthic macroinvertebrate community is impaired. Values of the USFS tolerance quotient range from 20 to just over 100, with lower values indicating better water quality. It should be noted that the Mill Creek macroinvertebrate sample scored better on the USFS community tolerance quotient than Doan Creek (96).

The number of Ephemeroptera, Plecoptera, Trichoptera (EPT) taxa was 9; there were 4 long lived taxa; and the dominate family was Chironomidae (non-biting midges). These data along with the tolerance indices listed above suggest that, while Mill Creek is in better condition than Doan Creek, it is still impaired. Causes of impairment may be tied to elevated water temperatures, low dissolved oxygen levels and elevated pH. At the time this report was written, stream channel data from the UCBN's stream channel characteristics monitoring protocol were not available. However, these data may indicate that physical factors (substrate armoring, bank stabilization, etc.) are negatively impacting benthic assemblages.

The observed to expected ratio (OE) for this sample reach was 0.22 and indicated that Mill Creek was in "poor" condition. However, due to physiographic and climatic conditions at the sample location the model had to extrapolate rather than interpolate predictor variables. As a result the condition rating should be interpreted with caution. See Table 23 and Appendix F for additional summary metrics.

Table 23. Vital sign summary table for benthic macroinvertebrates in Mill Creek, 2011. Note that the entire macroinvertebrate taxa and metrics lists can be found in Appendix F and G.

Mill Creek Macroinvertebrate Summary August 2011	
PIBO Station	**3194**
Sample ID	**147161**
Richness*	21
Shannon's Diversity*	1.92
Simpson's Diversity*	0.73
Evenness*	0.63
# of EPT Taxa*	9
Dominant Family	Chironomidae
Dominant Taxa	Orthocladiinae
Hilsenhoff Biotic Index*	4.16
# of Intolerant Taxa*	2
# of Tolerant Taxa*	0
USFS Community Tolerance Quotient (d)*	88
# of shredder taxa*	2
# of scraper taxa*	1
# of collector-filterer taxa*	1
# of collector-gatherer taxa*	10
# of predator taxa*	2
# of clinger taxa*	5
Long-lived Taxa*	4

Coliform

Status:

The coliform sample from Mill Creek indicated that in early August 2011 *E. coli* levels (130/100 ml) fell below what is considered acceptable in adjacent states (<406/100ml for a single sample). State standards for bacteria are for fecal coliform rather than *E. coli*. (geometric mean of samples <200 cfu/100 ml, <10% of the samples can exceed 400 cfu/100 mL). At the time of sampling, the Walla Walla County health department was unable to run analysis for fecal coliform (Table 24).

Table 24. Results of the coliform sample taken from Mill Creek, August 2011.

Sample Date	Location	Total Coliform	*E. coli*
8/03/2011	Mill Creek– by Swegle Road	>1600/100 ml	130/100 ml

Literature Cited

Baldwin, K., D. Gray, and J. Jones. 2008. Walla Walla watershed PCBs, chlorinated pesticides, fecal coliform, temperature, pH and dissolved oxygen total maximum daily load- water quality implementation plan. No. 08-10-094. Washington Department of Ecology, Water Quality Program, Olympia, WA.

Baldwin, K., A. Stohr. 2007. Walla Walla watershed temperature total maximum daily load- water quality improvement report. No. 07-10-030. Washington Department of Ecology, Environmental Assessment Program and Water Quality Program, Olympia, WA.

Barbour, M. T., J. Gerritsen, B. D. Snyder, and J. B. Stribling. 1999. Rapid Bioassessment Protocols for Use in Streams and Wadeable Rivers: Periphyton, Benthic Macroinvertebrates and Fish, Second Edition. EPA 841-B-99-002. U.S. Environmental Protection Agency.

Bell, J., and D. Hinson. 2009. Natural resource condition assessment: Whitman Mission National Historic Site. Natural Resource Report NPS/UCBN/NRR-2009/118. National Park Service, Fort Collins, CO.

Garrett, L. K., T. J. Rodhouse, G. H. Dicus, C. C. Caudill, and M. R. Shardlow. 2007. Vitals Signs Monitoring Plan, Upper Columbia Basin Network. Natural Resource Report NPS/PWR/UCBN/NRR—2007/002. National Park Service, Fort Collins, CO.

Heitke, J. D., E. J. Archer, D. D. Dugaw, B. A. Bouwes, E. A. Archer, R. C. Henderson, J. L. Kershner. 2008. Effectiveness monitoring for streams and riparian areas: sampling protocol for stream channel attributes. PACFISH/INFISH- Biological Opinion Effectiveness Monitoroing Program (PIBO-EM). Logan, UT. (http://www.fs.fed.us/biology/fishecology/emp). Accessed 18 January 2010.

Hilsenhoff, W. L. 1987. An improved biotic index of organic stream pollution. Great Lakes Entomologist **20**:31-39.

Hilsenhoff, W. L. 1988. Rapid field assessment of organic pollution with a family-level biotic index. Journal of the North American Benthological Society, **7**:65–68.

Irwin, R. J. 2008. Draft Part B lite QA/QC review checklist for aquatic vital sign monitoring protocols and SOPs, National Park Service, Water Resources Division. Fort Collins, CO. (http://www.nature.nps.gov/water/Vital_Signs_Guidance/Guidance_Documents/PartBLite.pdf). Accessed 18 February 2010.

Joy, J., G. Pelletier, and K. Baldwin. 2007. Walla Walla river basin pH and dissolved oxygen total maximum daily load- water quality improvement report. No. 07-03-010. Washington Department of Ecology, Environmental Assessment Program and Water Quality Program, Olympia, WA.

Joy, J., T. Swanson, G. Donovan, J. Jones, and K. Baldwin. 2006. Walla Walla river basin fecal coliform bacteria total maximum daily load- water quality improvement report. No. 06-10-074. Washington Department of Ecology, Environmental Assessment Program and Water Quality Program, Olympia, WA.

McCullough, D. A. 1999. A review and synthesis of effects of alterations to the water temperature regime on freshwater life stages of salmonids, with special reference to chinook salmon. EPA 910-R-99-010. U.S. Environmental Protection Agency, Washington, DC.

National Park Service (NPS) 1997. Baseline water quality data inventory and analysis: Whitman Mission National Historic Site. NPS/NRWRD/NRTR-97/109. Fort Collins, CO.

National Park Service (NPS). 1999. Natural resource challenge: the National Park Service's action plan for preserving natural resources. US Department of the Interior, National Park Service, Washington D.C.

National Park Service (NPS). 2000. Strategic plan FY 2001-2005. NPS D-1383. US Department of the Interior National Park Service, Washington D.C. (http://planning.nps.gov/document/NPS_strategic_plan.pdf). Accessed 3 March 2011.

National Park Service (NPS). 2005. Whitman Mission National Historic Site- Doan Creek restoration project environmental assessment. US Department of the Interior, National Park Service, Washington D.C. http://www.nps.gov/whmi/parkmgmt/loader.cfm?csModule=security/getfile&PageID=11 3153. Accessed 13 January 2012.

Starkey, E. N. 2009. Upper Columbia Basin Network integrated water quality annual report 2008: Nez Perce National Historical Park (NEPE) and Whitman Mission National istoric Site (WHMI). Natural Resource Technical Report NPS/UCBN/NRTR—2009/214. National Park Service, Fort Collins, CO. (http://science.nature.nps.gov/im/units/ucbn/reports/index.cfm#IWQ_Mon). Accessed 4 January 2012.

Starkey, E. N., L. K. Garrett, T. J. Rodhouse, G. H. Dicus, and R. K. Steinhorst. 2008. Upper Columbia Basin Network integrated water quality monitoring protocol: Narrative version 1.0. Natural Resource Report NPS/UCBN/NRR—2008/026. National Park Service, Fort Collins, CO. (http://science.nature.nps.gov/im/units/ucbn/reports/index.cfm#IWQ_Mon). Accessed 4 January 2012.

Stohr, A., M. LeMoine, and G. Pelletier. 2007. Walla Walla river tributaries temperature total maximum daily load study. No. 07-03-014. Washington Department of Ecology, Environmental Assessment Program, Olympia, WA.

United States Army Corps of Engineers (USACE). 1995a. Mill Creek master plan, main report. Vol1.

United States Army Corps of Engineers (USACE). 1995b. Mill Creek master plan, main report. Vol2.

United States EPA. 2001. Environmental Monitoring and Assessment Program (EMAP): National Coastal Assessment Quality Assurance Project Plan 2001-2004. United States Environmental Protection Agency, Office of Research and Development, National Health and Environmental Effects Research Laboratory, Gulf Ecology Division, Gulf Breeze, FL.EPA/620/R-01/002.

United States EPA. 1995. Environmental Monitoring and Assessment Program (EMAP): Laboratory Methods Manual-Estuaries, Volume 1: Biological and Physical Analyses. U.S. Environmental Protection Agency, Office of Research and Development , Narragansett, RI. EPA/620/R-95/008.

Vannote, R. L., and B. W. Sweeney. 1980. Geographic analysis of thermal equilibria: a conceptual model for evaluating the effect of natural and modified thermal regimes on aquatic insect communities. The American Naturalist **115:** 667–695.

Wagner, R. J., R. W. Boulger Jr., C. J. Oblinger, and B. A. Smith. 2006. Guidelines and Standard procedures for continuous water-quality monitors: station operation, record computation, and data reporting: U.S. Geological Survey Techniques and Methods 1–D3, 51.

Walla Walla County Conservation District (WWCCD). 2008. Doan Creek restoration project phase 1 and 2 final report. Walla Walla County Conservation District, Walla Walla, WA.

Washington Administrative Code. 2011. Washington administrative code-water quality standards for surface waters of the state of Washington. Chapter 173-201A WAC. . Washington Department of Ecology, Olympia, WA. (http://www.ecy.wa.gov/pubs/wac173201a.pdf). Accessed 12 January 2012.

Washington Department of Ecology. 2008. Water quality assessment 305 (b) report and 303(d) list. Available from http://apps.ecy.wa.gov/wats08/ (accessed 13 January 2012).

Appendix A. 2009-2011 Water Quality Monitoring Locations

Whitman Mission National Historical Park
Doan Creek
Washington

National Park Service
U.S. Department of the Interior

WHMI- Water Quality Monitoring 2010

Streamflow

- ○ Doan Creek Hydrolab Station 01
- Doan Creek
- WHMI NPS Boundary

0   100   200
Meters

Produced by the Upper Columbia Basin Network

December 2011

Appendix A. 2009-2011 Water Quality Monitoring Locations (continued)

Whitman Mission National Historical Park
Mill Creek
Washington

National Park Service
U.S. Department of the Interior

WHMI- Water Quality Monitoring 2009 and 2011

Streamflow

○   Mill Creek Hydrolab Station 01

⋀   Mill Creek

☐   WHMI NPS Boundary

N

0   100   200
Meters

Produced by the Upper Columbia Basin Network

December 2011

Appendix B. WHMI Hydrologic Unit Code Boundaries

Whitman Mission National Historical Park
Washington

National Park Service
U.S. Department of the Interior

Hydrologic Unit Code Boundaries

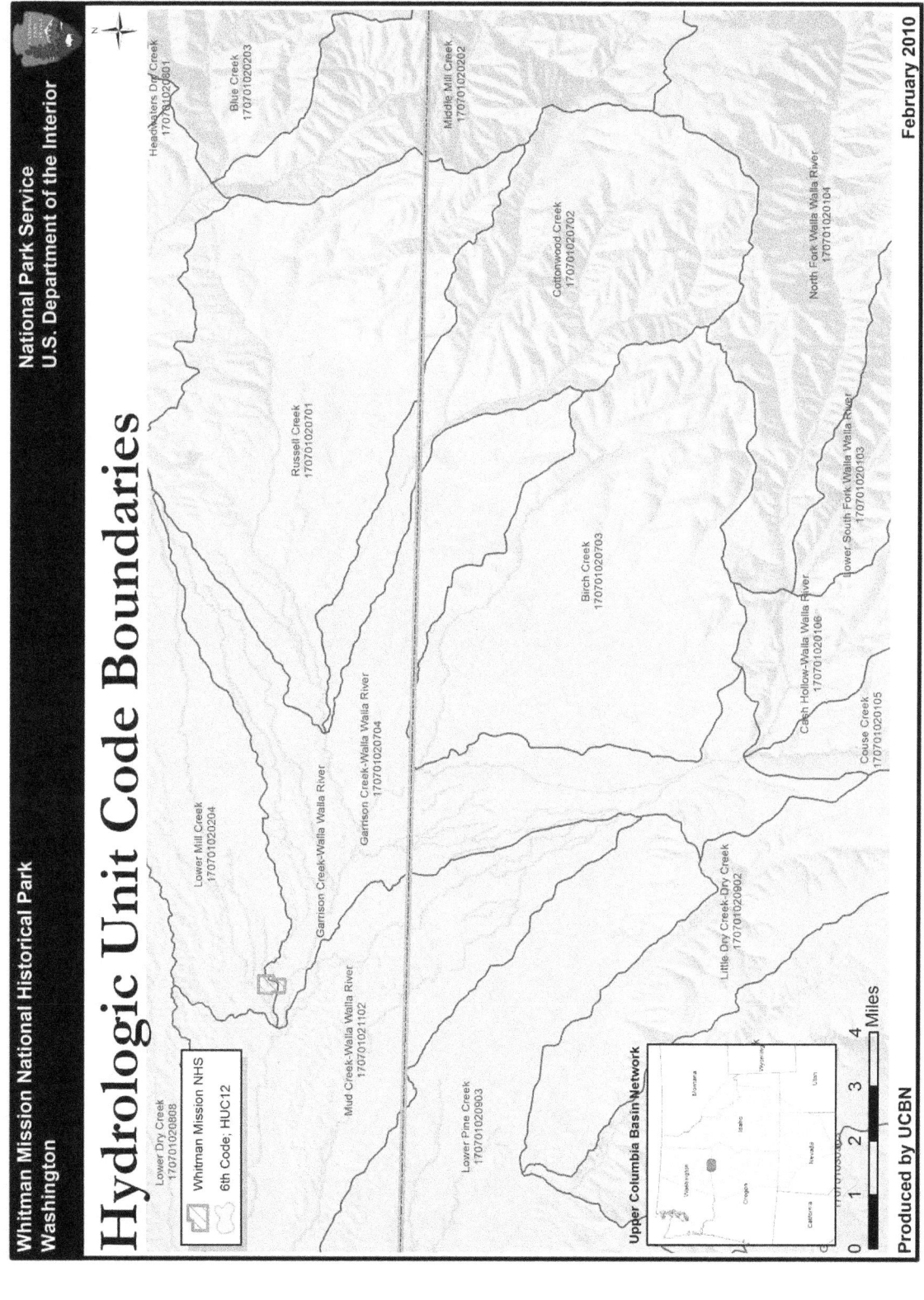

Legend:
- Whitman Mission NHS
- 6th Code; HUC12

Lower Dry Creek
170701020808

Lower Mill Creek
170701020204

Garrison Creek-Walla Walla River

Mud Creek-Walla Walla River
170701021102

Russell Creek
170701020701

Garrison Creek-Walla Walla River
170701020704

Lower Pine Creek
170701020903

Headwaters Dry Creek
170701020601

Blue Creek
170701020203

Middle Mill Creek
170701020202

Cottonwood Creek
170701020702

Birch Creek
170701020703

North Fork Walla Walla River
170701020104

Cash Hollow-Walla Walla River
170701020106

Lower South Fork Walla Walla River
170701020103

Little Dry Creek-Dry Creek
170701020902

Couse Creek
170701020105

Upper Columbia Basin Network

0 1 2 3 4 Miles

Produced by UCBN

February 2010

63

Appendix C. Sample Locations for Water Quality Monitoring at WHMI

Park	Stream	Monitoring Type	Station #	Lat.	Long.	Y	X
WHMI	Doan Creek	Water Chemistry	001	46.044167	-118.463377	5099996	386778
WHMI	Mill Creek	Water Chemistry	001	46.04366488	-118.46517032	5099943	386638
WHMI	Doan Creek	Macroinvertebrates	3195	46.04414805	-118.4604884	5099990	387001
WHMI	Mill Creek	Macroinvertebrates	3194	46.04218851	-118.4687082	5099784	386361

Note that X and Y have been projected in WGS84, UTM Zone 11. These locations were recorded by the field crew with a handheld GPS unit.

Appendix D. Quality Control (QC) Indicators

QC data quality indicators for 2009 season at WHMI- Mill Creek, Hydrolab #095, Station ID: WHMI-Mill #001.

STORET Name	Units	Detection Range Description from Manufacture	Method Detection Limit (MDL)	Minimum Level of Quantitation (ML)	Alternative Measurement Sensitivity Plus (AMS+) Beginning of Season	Alternative Measurement Sensitivity Plus (AMS+) End of Season	Precision+ (RPD) Beginning of Season	Precision+ (RPD) End of Season
Temperature, water	deg C	-5 to 50°C	N/A	N/A	0.55	Undetermined	0.00	Undetermined
Specific Conductance	µS/cm	0 to 100,000 µS/cm	N/A	N/A	0.8	→	0.50	→
Dissolved Oxygen	mg/L	0-20 mg/L	N/A	N/A	0.67		0.00	
pH	pH units	0-14 Units	N/A	N/A	0.11		0.00	
Turbidity	NTU	0-3000 NTU	0.1	0.38	0.2		10.53	

QC data quality indicators for 2010 season at WHMI-Doan Creek Hydrolab #095, Station ID: WHMI-Doan #001.

STORET Name	Units	Detection Range Description from Manufacture	Method Detection Limit (MDL)	Minimum Level of Quantitation (ML)	Alternative Measurement Sensitivity Plus (AMS+) Beginning of Season	Alternative Measurement Sensitivity Plus (AMS+) End of Season	Precision+ (RPD) Beginning of Season	Precision+ (RPD) End of Season
Temperature, water	deg C	-5 to 50°C	N/A	N/A	0.22	0.01	0.22	0.00
Specific Conductance	µS/cm	0 to 100,000 µS/cm	N/A	N/A	0.6	0.4	0.51	0.05
Dissolved Oxygen	mg/L	0-20 mg/L	N/A	N/A	0.08	0.06	0.09	0.00
pH	pH units	0-14 Units	N/A	N/A	0.25	0.46	0.51	0.53
Turbidity	NTU	0-3000 NTU	0.3	0.90	1.8	0.5	9.17	12.50

Appendix D. Quality Control (QC) Indicators (continued)

QC data quality indicators for 2011 season at WHMI-Mill Creek Hydrolab #095, Station ID: WHMI-Mill #001.

STORET Name	Units	Detection Range Description from Manufacture	Method Detection Limit (MDL)	Minimum Level of Quantitation (ML)	Alternative Measurement Sensitivity Plus (AMS+) Beginning of Season	Alternative Measurement Sensitivity Plus (AMS+) End of Season	Precision+ (RPD) Beginning of Season	Precision+ (RPD) End of Season
Temperature, water	deg C	-5 to 50°C	N/A	N/A	0.03	0.03	0.05	0.12
Specific Conductance	µS/cm	0 to 100,000 µS/cm	N/A	N/A	0.7	0.4	0.00	0.13
Dissolved Oxygen	mg/L	0-20 mg/L	N/A	N/A	0.02	Undetermined	0.11	Undetermined
pH	pH units	0-14 Units	N/A	N/A	0.02	0.02	0.12	0.26
Turbidity	NTU	0-3000 NTU	0.6	1.86	17.8	Undetermined	7.63	Undetermined

68

Appendix E. Corrections History

Correction history for Mill Creek, WHMI 2009 temperature data.

Creator	Comment	From Time	To Time	Applied Time	Points Modified
EStarkey	Delete region due to low battery power	7/13/2009 17:45	7/21/2009 21:45	8/4/2009 9:45	51
EStarkey	Delete Region	7/16/2009 0:45	7/16/2009 8:45	3/16/2011 11:54	4
EStarkey	Delete region due to loss of battery power. Note: data also deleted upon import due to improper date/time stamp given when battery power was zero. In addition no late turn on recorded from 8/13 to 8/25 assumption is that the battery was completely dead.	8/12/2009 5:00	8/12/2009 15:00	9/8/2009 10:32	7
EStarkey	Drift Correction with Calibration Drift value of 0.000 and Fouling Drift value of 0.000 °C. No correction applied. Site inspection indicates correction needed, due to changes in water temp during cleaning.	7/22/2009 5:00	8/12/2009 4:00	9/8/2009 10:35	504
EStarkey	Delete region due to outlier	7/22/2009 5:00	7/22/2009 5:00	9/8/2009 10:38	1
EStarkey	Delete Region	8/12/2009 15:00	8/12/2009 15:00	3/16/2011 11:54	1
EStarkey	Delete region due to low battery	9/20/2009 22:30	9/25/2009 8:30	10/2/2009 8:12	103
EStarkey	Delete Region	9/24/2009 1:30	9/25/2009 8:30	3/16/2011 11:55	28
EStarkey	Delete point(s)	11/1/2009 2:00	11/1/2009 2:00	3/16/2011 11:49	1
EStarkey	Clock Dift Correction with start offset of -60.000 and end offset of -60.000. Due to change from PDT to PST.	11/1/2009 3:00	11/24/2009 11:00	3/16/2011 11:51	561
EStarkey	Delete region due to low battery power	7/13/2009 17:45	7/21/2009 21:45	8/4/2009 9:45	51

Correction history for Mill Creek, WHMI 2009 specific conductance data.

Creator	Comment	From Time	To Time	Applied Time	Points Modified
EStarkey	Delete region due to low battery power	7/13/2009 17:45	7/21/2009 21:45	8/4/2009 9:52	51
EStarkey	Delete region due to outlier	7/12/2009 9:45	7/12/2009 9:45	8/4/2009 9:53	1
EStarkey	Delete region due to outlier	7/7/2009 9:45	7/7/2009 9:45	8/4/2009 9:53	1
EStarkey	Delete region due to outlier	7/12/2009 17:45	7/12/2009 17:45	8/4/2009 9:54	1
EStarkey	Delete Region	7/16/2009 0:45	7/16/2009 8:45	3/16/2011 13:14	4
EStarkey	Delete region due to outlier	7/24/2009 2:00	7/24/2009 2:00	9/8/2009 10:42	1
EStarkey	Delete region due to outlier	7/26/2009 0:00	7/26/2009 0:00	9/8/2009 10:42	1

Appendix E. Corrections History (continued)

Correction history for Mill Creek, WHMI 2009 specific conductance data (continued).

Creator	Comment	From Time	To Time	Applied Time	Points Modified
EStarkey	Delete region due to loss of battery power. Note: data also deleted upon import due to improper date/time stamp given when battery power was zero. In addition no late turn on recorded from 8/13 to 8/25 assumption is that the battery was completely dead.	8/12/2009 5:00	8/12/2009 15:00	9/8/2009 10:43	7
EStarkey	Drift Correction with Calibration Drift value of -0.060 and Fouling Drift value of -1.4 µS/cm	7/22/2009 5:00	8/12/2009 4:00	9/8/2009 10:44	504
EStarkey	Delete Region	8/12/2009 15:00	8/12/2009 15:00	3/16/2011 13:14	1
EStarkey	Delete region due to low battery	9/20/2009 22:30	9/25/2009 8:30	10/2/2009 8:17	103
EStarkey	Delete region due to outlier	9/1/2009 14:30	9/1/2009 14:30	10/2/2009 8:19	1
EStarkey	Delete region due to outlier	9/9/2009 15:30	9/9/2009 15:30	10/2/2009 8:21	1
EStarkey	Drift Correction with Calibration Drift value of 6.100 and Fouling Drift value of -1.3 µS/cm	8/26/2009 17:30	9/20/2009 21:30	10/2/2009 8:27	605
EStarkey	Delete Region	9/24/2009 1:30	9/25/2009 8:30	3/16/2011 13:14	28
EStarkey	Drift Correction with Calibration Drift value of -0.030 and Fouling Drift value of -.1 µS/cm	9/25/2009 18:00	10/16/2009 11:00	11/3/2009 14:26	498
EStarkey	Delete point(s)	11/1/2009 2:00	11/1/2009 2:00	3/16/2011 13:10	1
EStarkey	Clock Dift Correction with start offset of -60.000 and end offset of -60.000 Due to change from PDT to PST	11/1/2009 3:00	11/24/2009 11:00	3/16/2011 13:12	561

Correction history for Mill Creek, WHMI 2009 dissolved oxygen data.

Creator	Comment	From Time	To Time	Applied Time	Points Modified
EStarkey	Delete region due to outlier	7/12/2009 18:45	7/16/2009 8:45	8/4/2009 9:57	73
EStarkey	Delete Region	7/15/2009 22:45	7/16/2009 8:45	3/16/2011 13:34	5
EStarkey	Delete Region	7/21/2009 21:45	7/21/2009 21:45	3/16/2011 13:36	1
EStarkey	Delete region due to low battery power	8/12/2009 5:00	8/12/2009 15:00	9/8/2009 10:47	7

Appendix E. Corrections History (continued)

Correction history for Mill Creek, WHMI 2009 dissolved oxygen data (continued).

Creator	Comment	From Time	To Time	Applied Time	Points Modified
EStarkey	Drift Correction with Calibration Drift value of 0.000 and Fouling Drift value of -.06 mg/l. NOTE: possible error in after cleaning D.O. value. Data is within the range of values last year during similar temps. Correction applied only for drift. Rating will be upgraded to fair.	7/22/2009 5:00	8/12/2009 4:00	9/8/2009 10:55	504
EStarkey	Delete Region	8/12/2009 15:00	8/12/2009 15:00	3/16/2011 13:34	1
EStarkey	Delete region due to low battery	9/19/2009 21:30	9/25/2009 8:30	10/2/2009 8:23	128
EStarkey	Drift Correction with Calibration Drift value of 0.070 and Fouling Drift value of 0.42 mg/l	8/26/2009 17:30	9/19/2009 20:30	10/2/2009 8:25	580
EStarkey	Delete Region	9/23/2009 23:30	9/25/2009 8:30	3/16/2011 13:35	30
EStarkey	Delete region due to outlier	10/11/2009 17:00	10/11/2009 18:00	11/3/2009 14:30	2
EStarkey	Delete region due to outlier	11/10/2009 9:00	11/10/2009 9:00	12/1/2009 10:17	1
EStarkey	Delete region due to outlier/low battery	11/24/2009 1:00	11/24/2009 11:00	12/1/2009 10:18	11
EStarkey	Delete point(s)	11/1/2009 2:00	11/1/2009 2:00	3/16/2011 13:31	1
EStarkey	Clock Dift Correction with start offset of -60.000 and end offset of -60.000 Due to shift from PDT to PST	11/1/2009 3:00	11/24/2009 0:00	3/16/2011 13:32	550

Correction history for Mill Creek, WHMI 2009 pH data.

Creator	Comment	From Time	To Time	Applied Time	Points Modified
EStarkey	Delete region due to low battery power	7/13/2009 17:45	7/21/2009 21:45	8/4/2009 10:01	51
EStarkey	Delete Region	7/16/2009 0:45	7/16/2009 8:45	3/16/2011 14:01	4
EStarkey	Delete region due to loss of battery power. Note: data also deleted upon import due to improper date/time stamp given when battery power was zero. In addition no late turn on recorded from 8/13 to 8/25 assumption is that the battery was completely dead.	8/12/2009 5:00	8/12/2009 15:00	9/8/2009 10:57	7
EStarkey	Drift Correction with Calibration Drift value of -0.150 and Fouling Drift value of .29 Units	7/22/2009 5:00	8/12/2009 4:00	9/8/2009 10:58	504
EStarkey	Delete Region	8/12/2009 15:00	8/12/2009 15:00	3/16/2011 14:01	1

Appendix E. Corrections History (continued)

Correction history for Mill Creek, WHMI 2009 pH data (continued).

Creator	Comment	From Time	To Time	Applied Time	Points Modified
EStarkey	Delete region due to low battery	9/20/2009 22:30	9/25/2009 8:30	10/2/2009 8:28	103
EStarkey	Delete Region	9/24/2009 1:30	9/25/2009 8:30	3/16/2011 14:02	28
EStarkey	Delete point(s)	11/1/2009 2:00	11/1/2009 2:00	3/16/2011 13:57	1
EStarkey	Clock Dift Correction with start offset of -60.000 and end offset of -60.000 Due to switch from PDT to PST	11/1/2009 3:00	11/24/2009 11:00	3/16/2011 13:59	561

Correction history for Mill Creek, WHMI 2009 turbidity data.

Creator	Comment	From Time	To Time	Applied Time	Points Modified
EStarkey	Delete region due to low battery power	7/13/2009 3:45	7/21/2009 21:45	8/4/2009 10:04	65
EStarkey	Delete region due to outlier	7/10/2009 13:45	7/10/2009 13:45	8/4/2009 10:06	1
EStarkey	Delete region due to outlier	7/3/2009 23:45	7/3/2009 23:45	8/4/2009 10:06	1
EStarkey	Delete region due to outlier	6/25/2009 12:45	6/25/2009 12:45	8/4/2009 10:07	1
EStarkey	Delete region due to outlier	7/6/2009 14:45	7/6/2009 14:45	8/4/2009 10:10	1
EStarkey	Delete region	7/1/2009 14:45	7/1/2009 14:45	8/4/2009 10:10	1
EStarkey	Delete region due to outlier	6/23/2009 14:45	6/23/2009 14:45	8/4/2009 10:10	1
EStarkey	Preprocessing Horizontal Trim	6/19/2009 14:45	7/21/2009 21:45	8/4/2009 10:11	630
EStarkey	Delete region due to loss of battery power. Note: data also deleted upon import due to improper date/time stamp given when battery power was zero. In addition no late turn on recorded from 8/13 to 8/25 assumption is that the battery was completely dead.	8/12/2009 5:00	8/12/2009 15:00	9/8/2009 11:01	7
EStarkey	Delete region due to outlier	7/24/2009 2:00	7/24/2009 2:00	9/8/2009 11:01	1
EStarkey	Delete region due to outlier	7/25/2009 3:00	7/25/2009 3:00	9/8/2009 11:01	1
EStarkey	Delete region due to outlier	7/26/2009 4:00	7/26/2009 4:00	9/8/2009 11:02	1
EStarkey	Delete region due to outlier	7/27/2009 7:00	7/27/2009 7:00	9/8/2009 11:02	1
EStarkey	Delete region due to outlier	8/2/2009 13:00	8/2/2009 13:00	9/8/2009 11:02	1
EStarkey	Delete Region	8/5/2009 16:00	8/5/2009 16:00	9/8/2009 11:03	1
EStarkey	Delete region due to outlier	8/6/2009 11:00	8/6/2009 11:00	9/8/2009 11:03	1
EStarkey	Delete region due to outlier	8/7/2009 21:00	8/7/2009 21:00	9/8/2009 11:03	1
EStarkey	Delete region due to outlier	8/8/2009 10:00	8/8/2009 10:00	9/8/2009 11:03	1
EStarkey	Delete region due to outlier	8/10/2009 15:00	8/10/2009 15:00	9/8/2009 11:04	1
EStarkey	Delete region due to outlier	8/11/2009 15:00	8/11/2009 15:00	9/8/2009 11:04	1

Appendix E. Corrections History (continued)

Correction history for Mill Creek, WHMI 2009 turbidity data (continued).

Creator	Comment	From Time	To Time	Applied Time	Points Modified
EStarkey	Delete region due to low battery	9/18/2009 21:30	9/25/2009 8:30	10/2/2009 8:32	152
EStarkey	Delete region due to outlier	9/5/2009 23:30	9/5/2009 23:30	10/2/2009 8:32	1
EStarkey	Drift Correction with Calibration Drift value of 1.000 and Fouling Drift value of 0 NTU	8/26/2009 17:30	9/18/2009 20:30	10/2/2009 8:33	556
EStarkey	Delete region due to outlier	9/28/2009 7:00	9/28/2009 7:00	11/3/2009 14:34	1
EStarkey	Drift Correction with Calibration Drift value of 0.000 and Fouling Drift value of 0.000 NTU. Site Inspection Summary form indicates that a -1.1 correction should be applied. To avoid negative turbidity values this was not applied.	9/25/2009 18:00	10/16/2009 11:00	11/3/2009 15:00	498
EStarkey	Delete region due to outlier	11/4/2009 23:00	11/4/2009 23:00	12/1/2009 10:24	1
EStarkey	Delete region due to low battery power	7/13/2009 3:45	7/21/2009 21:45	8/4/2009 10:04	65
EStarkey	Delete region due to outlier	11/5/2009 13:00	11/5/2009 14:00	12/1/2009 10:24	2
EStarkey	Delete region due to outlier	11/13/2009 11:00	11/13/2009 11:00	12/1/2009 10:25	1
EStarkey	Delete region due to outlier	11/13/2009 20:00	11/13/2009 20:00	12/1/2009 10:25	1
EStarkey	Delete region due to outlier	11/2/2009 11:00	11/2/2009 11:00	12/1/2009 10:27	1
EStarkey	Delete region due to outlier	11/5/2009 11:00	11/5/2009 11:00	12/1/2009 10:28	1
EStarkey	Delete region due to outlier	11/7/2009 15:00	11/7/2009 15:00	12/1/2009 10:28	1
EStarkey	Delete region due to outlier	11/7/2009 23:00	11/7/2009 23:00	12/1/2009 10:28	1
EStarkey	Delete region due to outlier	11/18/2009 17:00	11/18/2009 17:00	12/1/2009 10:29	1
EStarkey	Delete region due to outlier	11/20/2009 20:00	11/20/2009 20:00	12/1/2009 10:29	1
EStarkey	Delete region due to outlier	11/21/2009 1:00	11/21/2009 1:00	12/1/2009 10:29	1
EStarkey	Delete region due to outlier	11/21/2009 23:00	11/21/2009 23:00	12/1/2009 10:30	1
EStarkey	Delete region due to outlier	11/22/2009 19:00	11/22/2009 19:00	12/1/2009 10:30	1
EStarkey	Delete region due to outlier	11/22/2009 22:00	11/22/2009 22:00	12/1/2009 10:30	1
EStarkey	Delete region due to outlier	11/23/2009 8:00	11/23/2009 8:00	12/1/2009 10:31	1
EStarkey	Delete region due to outlier	11/23/2009 11:00	11/23/2009 11:00	12/1/2009 10:31	1
EStarkey	Delete point(s)	11/1/2009 2:00	11/1/2009 2:00	3/16/2011 14:30	1
EStarkey	Clock Dift Correction with start offset of -60.000 and end offset of -60.000 Due to time change PDT to PST	11/1/2009 3:00	11/24/2009 11:00	3/16/2011 14:32	561

Appendix E. Corrections History (continued)

Correction history for Doan Creek, WHMI 2010 temperature data.

Creator	Comment	From Time	To Time	Applied Time	Points Modified
EStarkey	Delete Region due to low battery	5/12/2010 1:30	5/12/2010 1:30	5/28/2010 8:54	1
EStarkey	Delete Region due to low battery	5/12/2010 4:30	5/12/2010 7:30	5/28/2010 8:55	4
EStarkey	Delete Region due to low battery	5/12/2010 10:30	5/12/2010 10:30	5/28/2010 8:56	1
EStarkey	Delete Region due to low battery	5/12/2010 22:30	5/14/2010 13:30	5/28/2010 8:56	33
EStarkey	Delete Region due to low battery	6/12/2010 7:16	6/12/2010 9:03	7/7/2010 13:45	2
EStarkey	Delete Region due to low battery	6/12/2010 22:58	6/18/2010 4:22	7/7/2010 13:45	65
EStarkey	Delete Region due to low battery	6/21/2010 22:43	6/29/2010 14:16	9/2/2010 15:14	173
EStarkey	Delete Region due to low battery	9/15/2010 23:10	9/22/2010 7:30	10/4/2010 9:54	115
EStarkey	Delete Region due to low battery	10/12/2010 9:14	10/14/2010 10:00	10/15/2010 10:06	43
EStarkey	Delete Region due to low battery	11/2/2010 6:05	11/5/2010 2:30	11/18/2010 8:37	52
EStarkey	Clock Dift Correction with start offset of -60.000 and end offset of -60.000 Change from PDT to PST.	11/10/2010 19:00	11/19/2010 9:00	3/17/2011 9:30	207

Correction history for Doan Creek, WHMI 2010 specific conductance data.

Creator	Comment	From Time	To Time	Applied Time	Points Modified
EStarkey	Delete Region due to low battery	5/12/2010 1:30	5/12/2010 1:30	5/28/2010 9:38	1
EStarkey	Delete Region due to low battery	5/12/2010 4:30	5/12/2010 7:30	5/28/2010 9:39	4
EStarkey	Delete Region due to low battery	5/12/2010 10:30	5/12/2010 10:30	5/28/2010 9:39	1
EStarkey	Delete Region due to low battery	5/12/2010 22:30	5/13/2010 11:30	5/28/2010 9:39	13
EStarkey	Delete Region due to low battery	5/13/2010 19:30	5/14/2010 13:30	5/28/2010 9:40	16
EStarkey	Delete Region due to low battery	6/12/2010 7:30	6/12/2010 9:30	7/7/2010 13:48	2
EStarkey	Delete Region due to low battery	6/12/2010 22:43	6/18/2010 4:33	7/7/2010 13:49	65
EStarkey	Delete Region due to low battery, hydrolab sent in for repair due to issues with DO sensor and battery power	6/21/2010 22:06	6/29/2010 9:00	9/3/2010 8:53	173
EStarkey	Drift Correction with Calibration Drift value of 5.900 and Fouling Drift value of 8.950	7/19/2010 15:00	8/5/2010 12:00	9/3/2010 9:05	406
EStarkey	Delete Region due to low battery	9/15/2010 22:17	9/22/2010 7:30	10/4/2010 9:57	115
EStarkey	Drift Correction with Calibration Drift value of 8.200 and Fouling Drift value of 33.000	8/26/2010 15:30	9/22/2010 7:30	10/4/2010 9:59	487
EStarkey	Delete Region due to low battery	10/12/2010 9:38	10/14/2010 11:04	10/15/2010 10:08	43
EStarkey	Delete Region due to outlier	9/25/2010 19:53	9/25/2010 20:08	10/15/2010 10:09	1

Appendix E. Corrections History (continued)

Correction history for Doan Creek, WHMI 2010 specific conductance data (continued).

Creator	Comment	From Time	To Time	Applied Time	Points Modified
EStarkey	Drift Correction with Calibration Drift value of 5.150 and Fouling Drift value of 59.900	9/22/2010 16:00	10/14/2010 10:00	10/15/2010 10:11	472
EStarkey	Delete Region due to low battery	11/2/2010 5:21	11/5/2010 2:30	11/18/2010 8:44	52
EStarkey	Delete Region due to outlier	10/24/2010 11:05	10/24/2010 12:02	11/18/2010 8:45	1
EStarkey	Delete Region due to outlier	11/1/2010 12:30	11/1/2010 12:30	11/18/2010 8:45	1
EStarkey	Drift Correction with Calibration Drift value of -12.050 and Fouling Drift value of 7.900	10/14/2010 16:30	11/6/2010 7:53	11/18/2010 8:47	442
EStarkey	Delete Region due to outlier	11/14/2010 10:00	11/14/2010 10:00	11/29/2010 13:56	1
EStarkey	Delete Region due to outlier	11/17/2010 8:00	11/17/2010 8:00	11/29/2010 13:57	1
EStarkey	Delete Region due to outlier	11/17/2010 19:00	11/17/2010 19:00	11/29/2010 13:57	1

Correction history for Doan Creek, WHMI 2010 dissolved oxygen data.

Creator	Comment	From Time	To Time	Applied Time	Points Modified
EStarkey	Delete Region due to low battery	5/10/2010 5:30	5/14/2010 13:30	5/28/2010 9:49	95
EStarkey	Delete Region due to low battery	6/10/2010 2:00	6/18/2010 2:00	7/7/2010 13:52	132
EStarkey	Drift Correction with Calibration Drift value of -3.000 and Fouling Drift value of 0.000. Fouling correction was likely necessary but due to sensor error fouling could not be determined. For a more detailed description see the site inspection summary and maintenance log sheet.	5/24/2010 16:00	6/18/2010 14:10	7/7/2010 13:58	394
EStarkey	Delete Region, sensor failure. At the end of this deployment the instrument was returned to HACH for service	6/18/2010 17:00	6/29/2010 9:00	9/3/2010 9:11	251
EStarkey	Delete Region due to low battery	9/13/2010 20:44	9/22/2010 7:30	10/4/2010 10:01	164
EStarkey	Delete Region due to outlier	9/10/2010 16:30	9/10/2010 16:30	10/4/2010 10:02	1
EStarkey	Delete Region due to outlier	9/4/2010 4:30	9/4/2010 4:30	10/4/2010 10:02	1
EStarkey	Delete Region due to low battery	10/10/2010 22:26	10/14/2010 10:00	10/15/2010 10:12	77
EStarkey	Drift Correction with Calibration Drift value of -0.680 and Fouling Drift value of 0.170	9/22/2010 16:00	10/12/2010 6:00	10/15/2010 10:14	439
EStarkey	Delete Region due to outlier	9/30/2010 23:00	9/30/2010 23:00	10/15/2010 10:48	1
EStarkey	Delete Region due to low battery	10/31/2010 2:02	11/5/2010 2:30	11/18/2010 8:49	102

Appendix E. Corrections History (continued)

Correction history for Doan Creek, WHMI 2010 dissolved oxygen data (continued).

Creator	Comment	From Time	To Time	Applied Time	Points Modified
EStarkey	Delete Region due to outlier	10/19/2010 19:19	10/19/2010 19:44	11/18/2010 8:50	1
EStarkey	Delete Region due to outlier	10/23/2010 19:22	10/23/2010 19:43	11/18/2010 8:50	1
EStarkey	Delete Region due to outlier	11/16/2010 1:00	11/16/2010 1:00	11/29/2010 14:48	1
EStarkey	Delete Region due to outlier	11/17/2010 6:00	11/17/2010 6:00	11/29/2010 14:48	1
EStarkey	Delete Region due to outlier	11/17/2010 8:00	11/17/2010 8:00	11/29/2010 14:48	1
EStarkey	Clock Dift Correction with start offset of -60.000 and end offset of -60.000 Due to change from PDT to PST	11/10/2010 19:00	11/19/2010 9:00	3/17/2011 11:15	207

Correction history for Doan Creek, WHMI 2010 pH data.

Creator	Comment	From Time	To Time	Applied Time	Points Modified
EStarkey	Delete Region due to low battery	5/12/2010 1:30	5/12/2010 1:30	5/28/2010 10:04	1
EStarkey	Delete Region due to low battery	5/12/2010 4:30	5/12/2010 7:30	5/28/2010 10:04	4
EStarkey	Delete Region due to low battery	5/12/2010 10:30	5/12/2010 10:30	5/28/2010 10:04	1
EStarkey	Delete Region due to low battery	5/12/2010 22:30	5/13/2010 11:30	5/28/2010 10:04	13
EStarkey	Delete Region due to low battery	5/13/2010 19:30	5/14/2010 13:30	5/28/2010 10:05	16
EStarkey	Delete Region due to low battery	6/12/2010 7:24	6/12/2010 9:27	7/7/2010 14:00	2
EStarkey	Delete Region due to low battery	6/12/2010 23:01	6/18/2010 3:13	7/7/2010 14:00	65
EStarkey	Drift Correction with Calibration Drift value of -0.167 and Fouling Drift value of 0.130	5/24/2010 16:00	6/18/2010 13:47	7/7/2010 14:01	459
EStarkey	Delete Region due to low battery, D.O. sensor failure, instruement sent in for repair after this deployment	6/21/2010 22:07	6/29/2010 9:00	9/3/2010 9:17	173
EStarkey	Drift Correction with Calibration Drift value of -0.180 and Fouling Drift value of 0.153	7/19/2010 15:00	8/5/2010 12:00	9/3/2010 9:24	406
EStarkey	Delete Region due to low battery	9/15/2010 22:03	9/22/2010 7:30	10/4/2010 10:05	115
EStarkey	Drift Correction with Calibration Drift value of -0.113 and Fouling Drift value of -0.230	8/26/2010 15:30	9/18/2010 7:07	10/4/2010 10:06	487
EStarkey	Delete Region due to low battery	10/12/2010 7:36	10/14/2010 10:00	10/15/2010 10:15	44
EStarkey	Delete Region due to low battery	11/2/2010 5:24	11/5/2010 2:30	11/18/2010 8:53	52
EStarkey	Drift Correction with Calibration Drift value of -0.133 and Fouling Drift value of -0.080	10/14/2010 16:30	11/4/2010 5:45	11/18/2010 8:54	444

Appendix E. Corrections History (continued)

Correction history for Doan Creek, WHMI 2010 pH data (continued).

Creator	Comment	From Time	To Time	Applied Time	Points Modified
EStarkey	Drift Correction with Calibration Drift value of -0.067 and Fouling Drift value of -0.140	11/10/2010 19:00	11/19/2010 9:00	11/29/2010 14:54	207
EStarkey	Clock Dift Correction with start offset of -60.000 and end offset of -60.000 Due to change from PDT to PST	11/10/2010 19:00	11/19/2010 9:00	3/17/2011 11:41	207

Correction history for Doan Creek, WHMI 2010 turbidity data.

Creator	Comment	From Time	To Time	Applied Time	Points Modified
EStarkey	Delete Region due to low battery and wiper parking	5/9/2010 19:30	5/14/2010 13:30	5/28/2010 10:16	105
EStarkey	Delete Region due to outlier	4/27/2010 12:30	4/27/2010 12:30	5/28/2010 10:22	1
EStarkey	Delete Region due to outlier	4/29/2010 22:30	4/29/2010 22:30	5/28/2010 10:27	1
EStarkey	Delete Region due to outlier	4/23/2010 4:30	4/23/2010 4:30	5/28/2010 11:16	1
EStarkey	Delete Region due to outlier	4/21/2010 1:30	4/21/2010 1:30	5/31/2010 7:01	1
EStarkey	Delete Region due to outlier	4/21/2010 23:30	4/21/2010 23:30	5/31/2010 7:01	1
EStarkey	Delete Region due to outlier	5/6/2010 10:30	5/6/2010 10:30	5/31/2010 7:03	1
unknown		4/20/2010 14:30	5/14/2010 13:30	5/31/2010 14:03	0
EStarkey	Delete Region due to low battery	6/10/2010 2:00	6/18/2010 4:24	7/7/2010 14:04	132
EStarkey	Drift Correction with Calibration Drift value of -2.600 and Fouling Drift value of -2.600	5/24/2010 16:00	6/18/2010 21:53	7/7/2010 14:13	399
EStarkey	Delete Region due to outlier	6/3/2010 20:00	6/3/2010 20:00	9/3/2010 9:50	1
EStarkey	Delete Region due to outlier	6/5/2010 9:00	6/5/2010 9:00	9/3/2010 9:51	1
EStarkey	Delete Region due to outlier	6/8/2010 11:34	6/8/2010 13:12	9/3/2010 9:52	2
EStarkey	Delete Region due to outlier	6/8/2010 17:00	6/8/2010 17:00	9/3/2010 9:52	1
EStarkey	Delete Region due to outlier	6/8/2010 21:00	6/8/2010 21:00	9/3/2010 9:52	1
EStarkey	Delete Region due to outlier	6/9/2010 2:00	6/9/2010 2:00	9/3/2010 9:52	1
EStarkey	Delete Region due to outlier	6/9/2010 8:00	6/9/2010 8:00	9/3/2010 9:53	1
EStarkey	Delete Region due to outlier	6/4/2010 11:55	6/4/2010 14:14	9/3/2010 9:56	3
EStarkey	Delete Region due to outlier	6/5/2010 4:42	6/5/2010 6:30	9/3/2010 9:56	2
EStarkey	Delete Region due to outlier	6/5/2010 16:45	6/5/2010 20:30	9/3/2010 9:56	4
EStarkey	Delete Region due to outlier	6/6/2010 2:44	6/6/2010 3:33	9/3/2010 9:56	1
EStarkey	Delete Region due to outlier	6/6/2010 0:50	6/6/2010 1:21	9/3/2010 9:56	1
EStarkey	Delete Region due to outlier	6/6/2010 5:28	6/6/2010 7:37	9/3/2010 9:56	2

Appendix E. Corrections History (continued)

Correction history for Doan Creek, WHMI 2010 turbidity data (continued).

Creator	Comment	From Time	To Time	Applied Time	Points Modified
EStarkey	Delete Region due to low battery, D.O. sensor failure, hydrolab sent in for repair after this deployment	6/20/2010 20:00	6/29/2010 9:00	9/3/2010 9:33	200
EStarkey	Delete Region due to outlier	7/29/2010 6:00	7/29/2010 6:00	9/3/2010 9:40	1
EStarkey	Delete Region due to outlier	8/1/2010 14:00	8/1/2010 14:00	9/3/2010 9:40	1
EStarkey	Drift Correction with Calibration Drift value of -0.250 and Fouling Drift value of -0.500	7/19/2010 15:00	8/6/2010 3:24	9/3/2010 9:42	404
EStarkey	Delete Region due to outlier	8/27/2010 0:30	8/27/2010 0:30	10/4/2010 10:10	1
EStarkey	Delete Region due to outlier	8/31/2010 2:30	8/31/2010 2:30	10/4/2010 10:10	1
EStarkey	Delete Region due to outlier	9/2/2010 4:30	9/2/2010 5:30	10/4/2010 10:10	2
EStarkey	Delete Region due to outlier	9/16/2010 14:30	9/16/2010 14:30	10/4/2010 10:11	1
EStarkey	Delete Region due to low battery	9/15/2010 22:30	9/22/2010 7:30	10/4/2010 10:12	114
EStarkey	Delete Region due to low battery	10/12/2010 6:37	10/14/2010 10:00	10/15/2010 10:21	45
EStarkey	Delete Region due to outlier	10/4/2010 22:34	10/4/2010 23:41	10/15/2010 10:21	1
EStarkey	Delete Region due to outlier	10/5/2010 4:45	10/5/2010 5:20	10/15/2010 10:21	1
EStarkey	Delete Region due to outlier	10/3/2010 22:40	10/3/2010 23:30	10/15/2010 10:22	1
EStarkey	Delete Region due to outlier	9/29/2010 3:24	9/29/2010 4:23	10/15/2010 10:23	1
EStarkey	Delete Region due to outlier	10/8/2010 5:00	10/8/2010 5:00	10/15/2010 10:25	1
EStarkey	Delete Region due to outlier	10/12/2010 1:00	10/12/2010 1:00	10/15/2010 10:25	1
EStarkey	Delete Region due to low battery	11/2/2010 5:32	11/5/2010 2:30	11/18/2010 8:57	52
EStarkey	Delete Region due to outlier	11/1/2010 1:30	11/1/2010 1:30	11/18/2010 8:57	1
EStarkey	Delete Region due to outlier	10/31/2010 20:30	10/31/2010 20:30	11/18/2010 8:57	1
EStarkey	Delete Region due to outlier	10/31/2010 11:30	10/31/2010 11:30	11/18/2010 8:58	1
EStarkey	Delete Region due to outlier	10/15/2010 5:30	10/15/2010 5:30	11/18/2010 8:59	1
EStarkey	Delete Region due to outlier	11/11/2010 4:00	11/11/2010 4:00	11/29/2010 14:58	1
EStarkey	Delete Region due to outlier	11/11/2010 6:00	11/11/2010 6:00	11/29/2010 14:58	1
EStarkey	Delete Region due to outlier	11/11/2010 9:00	11/11/2010 9:00	11/29/2010 14:58	1
EStarkey	Delete Region due to outlier	11/12/2010 0:00	11/12/2010 0:00	11/29/2010 14:58	1
EStarkey	Delete Region due to outlier	11/12/2010 6:00	11/12/2010 6:00	11/29/2010 14:59	1
EStarkey	Delete Region due to outlier	11/16/2010 3:00	11/16/2010 3:00	11/29/2010 14:59	1
EStarkey	Delete Region due to outlier	11/15/2010 21:00	11/15/2010 21:00	11/29/2010 14:59	1
EStarkey	Delete Region due to outlier	11/18/2010 8:00	11/18/2010 9:00	11/29/2010 15:00	2
EStarkey	Delete Region due to outlier	11/19/2010 4:00	11/19/2010 4:00	11/29/2010 15:00	1

Appendix E. Corrections History (continued)

Correction history for Doan Creek, WHMI 2010 turbidity data (continued).

Creator	Comment	From Time	To Time	Applied Time	Points Modified
EStarkey	Clock Dift Correction with start offset of -60.000 and end offset of -60.000 Due to change from PDT to PST	11/10/2010 19:00	11/19/2010 9:00	3/17/2011 13:04	207

Correction history for Mill Creek, WHMI 2011 temperature data.

Creator	Comment	From Time	To Time	Applied Time	Points Modified
N/A	No Corrections Applied	N/A	N/A	N/A	0

Correction history for Mill Creek, WHMI 2011 specific conductance data.

Creator	Comment	From Time	To Time	Applied Time	Points Modified
EStarkey	Drift Correction with Calibration Drift value of -0.05µS/cm and Fouling Drift value of -6.40µS/cm	7/28/2011 15:15	8/24/2011 8:15	8/30/2011 15:05	642
EStarkey	Delete point(s)- due to outlier	9/4/2011 8:00	9/4/2011 8:00	9/26/2011 11:45	1
EStarkey	Delete Region- due to outlier	9/6/2011 4:00	9/6/2011 5:00	9/26/2011 11:45	2
EStarkey	Delete point(s)- due to outlier	9/6/2011 15:00	9/6/2011 15:00	9/26/2011 11:45	1
EStarkey	Delete point(s)- due to outlier	9/6/2011 23:00	9/6/2011 23:00	9/26/2011 11:46	1
EStarkey	Delete point(s)- due to outlier	9/8/2011 10:00	9/8/2011 10:00	9/26/2011 11:47	1
EStarkey	Delete point(s)- due to outlier	9/11/2011 21:00	9/11/2011 21:00	9/26/2011 11:47	1
EStarkey	Delete point(s)- due to outlier	9/13/2011 20:00	9/13/2011 20:00	9/26/2011 11:48	1
EStarkey	Delete point(s)- due to outlier	9/16/2011 22:00	9/16/2011 22:00	9/26/2011 11:49	1
EStarkey	Delete point(s)- due to outlier	9/18/2011 10:00	9/18/2011 10:00	9/26/2011 11:49	1
EStarkey	Delete point(s)- due to outlier	9/19/2011 18:00	9/19/2011 18:00	9/26/2011 11:55	1
EStarkey	Delete point(s)- due to outlier	9/20/2011 19:00	9/20/2011 19:00	9/26/2011 11:56	1
EStarkey	Delete point(s)- due to outlier	9/21/2011 10:00	9/21/2011 10:00	9/26/2011 11:56	1
EStarkey	Drift Correction with Calibration Drift value of 5.30µS/cm and Fouling Drift value of -4.25µS/cm	8/24/2011 16:00	9/22/2011 11:00	9/26/2011 11:58	679
EStarkey	Delete point(s)- due to outliers	9/6/2011 16:00	9/6/2011 17:00	11/15/2011 14:01	2
EStarkey	Delete Region- due to outlier	9/25/2011 15:30	9/25/2011 15:30	10/31/2011 12:31	1
EStarkey	Delete Region- due to outlier	9/28/2011 18:30	9/28/2011 18:30	10/31/2011 12:32	1
EStarkey	Delete point(s)- due to outlier	9/30/2011 1:30	9/30/2011 1:30	10/31/2011 12:32	1
EStarkey	Delete point(s)- due to outlier	9/30/2011 14:30	9/30/2011 14:30	10/31/2011 12:34	1
EStarkey	Delete Region- due to outlier	10/1/2011 18:30	10/1/2011 18:30	10/31/2011 12:34	1
EStarkey	Delete Region- due to outlier	10/1/2011 20:30	10/1/2011 20:30	10/31/2011 12:34	1
EStarkey	Delete Region- due to outlier	10/5/2011 18:30	10/5/2011 18:30	10/31/2011 12:35	1

Appendix E. Corrections History (continued)

Correction history for Mill Creek, WHMI 2011 specific conductance data (continued).

Creator	Comment	From Time	To Time	Applied Time	Points Modified
EStarkey	Delete Region- due to outlier	10/5/2011 16:30	10/5/2011 16:30	10/31/2011 12:35	1
EStarkey	Delete Region- due to outlier	10/6/2011 21:30	10/6/2011 21:30	10/31/2011 12:36	1
EStarkey	Delete Region- due to outlier	10/8/2011 5:30	10/8/2011 5:30	10/31/2011 12:36	1
EStarkey	Delete Region- due to outliers and suspected fouling	10/10/2011 16:30	10/10/2011 18:30	10/31/2011 12:37	3
EStarkey	Delete Region- due to outlier	10/12/2011 3:30	10/12/2011 3:30	10/31/2011 12:37	1
EStarkey	Delete Region- due to outlier	10/15/2011 6:30	10/15/2011 6:30	10/31/2011 12:38	1
EStarkey	Delete Region- due to outlier	10/15/2011 17:30	10/15/2011 17:30	10/31/2011 12:38	1

Correction history for Mill Creek, WHMI 2011 dissolved oxygen data.

Creator	Comment	From Time	To Time	Applied Time	Points Modified
AQ_AUTO	Remove flag Values for THRESHS type and 5 code	Open	Open	7/12/2011 8:43	107
EStarkey	Drift Correction with Calibration Drift value of -0.05mg/l and Fouling Drift value of 1.36mg/l	7/28/2011 15:15	8/24/2011 8:15	8/30/2011 15:08	642
EStarkey	Delete point(s)- due to outlier	9/20/2011 21:00	9/20/2011 21:00	9/26/2011 14:18	1
EStarkey	Delete point(s)- due to outlier	9/13/2011 7:00	9/13/2011 7:00	9/26/2011 14:18	1
EStarkey	Drift Correction with Calibration Drift value of -0.11mg/l and Fouling Drift value of 0.49mg/l	8/24/2011 16:00	9/22/2011 11:00	9/26/2011 14:20	690
EStarkey	Delete Region- due to outlier	10/10/2011 5:30	10/10/2011 5:30	10/31/2011 12:48	1
EStarkey	Delete Region- due to outlier	10/12/2011 15:30	10/12/2011 15:30	10/31/2011 12:48	1
EStarkey	Delete Region- due to outliers	10/13/2011 10:30	10/13/2011 12:30	10/31/2011 12:48	3
EStarkey	Delete Region- due to outlier	9/25/2011 19:30	9/25/2011 19:30	10/31/2011 12:49	1
EStarkey	Drift Correction with Calibration Drift value of -0.07mg/l and Fouling Drift value of 0.77mg/l	9/22/2011 16:30	10/19/2011 11:30	10/31/2011 12:51	638
EStarkey	Delete Region- due to sensor failure	10/26/2011 12:30	11/8/2011 9:30	11/15/2011 14:04	310

Correction history for Mill Creek, WHMI 2011 pH data.

Creator	Comment	From Time	To Time	Applied Time	Points Modified
EStarkey	Drift Correction with Calibration Drift value of 0.11pH Units and Fouling Drift value of 0.12pH Units	8/24/2011 16:00	9/22/2011 11:00	9/26/2011 14:24	692

Appendix E. Corrections History (continued)

Correction history for Mill Creek, WHMI 2011 turbidity data.

Creator	Comment	From Time	To Time	Applied Time	Points Modified
EStarkey	Delete point(s)- Due to outlier	7/2/2011 15:00	7/2/2011 15:00	7/12/2011 8:49	1
EStarkey	Delete point(s)- Due to outlier	6/25/2011 14:00	6/25/2011 14:00	7/12/2011 8:50	1
EStarkey	Delete Region- due to outlier	8/17/2011 11:15	8/17/2011 11:15	8/30/2011 15:20	1
EStarkey	Delete Region- due to outlier	8/19/2011 7:15	8/19/2011 7:15	8/30/2011 15:21	1
EStarkey	Delete Region- due to outlier	8/19/2011 17:15	8/19/2011 17:15	8/30/2011 15:21	1
EStarkey	Delete Region- due to outlier	8/20/2011 10:15	8/20/2011 10:15	8/30/2011 15:21	1
EStarkey	Delete Region- due to outlier	8/20/2011 12:15	8/20/2011 12:15	8/30/2011 15:21	1
EStarkey	Delete Region- due to outlier	8/20/2011 14:15	8/20/2011 14:15	8/30/2011 15:22	1
EStarkey	Delete Region- due to outlier	8/21/2011 12:15	8/21/2011 12:15	8/30/2011 15:22	1
EStarkey	Delete Region- due to outlier	8/22/2011 7:15	8/22/2011 7:15	8/30/2011 15:22	1
EStarkey	Delete Region- due to outlier	8/22/2011 9:15	8/22/2011 9:15	8/30/2011 15:22	1
EStarkey	Delete Region- due to outliers	8/17/2011 14:15	8/17/2011 15:15	9/12/2011 14:22	2
EStarkey	Delete Region- due to outliers	8/18/2011 9:15	8/18/2011 11:15	9/12/2011 14:23	3
EStarkey	Delete Region- due to outlier	8/21/2011 6:15	8/21/2011 6:15	9/12/2011 14:23	1
EStarkey	Delete Region- due to outlier	8/21/2011 17:15	8/21/2011 17:15	9/12/2011 14:23	1
EStarkey	Delete point(s)- due to outlier	8/22/2011 8:15	8/22/2011 8:15	9/12/2011 14:26	1
EStarkey	Delete Region- due to outlier	8/20/2011 11:15	8/20/2011 13:15	9/12/2011 14:26	2
EStarkey	Delete point(s)- due to outlier	8/3/2011 13:15	8/3/2011 13:15	9/12/2011 14:34	1
EStarkey	Delete point(s)- due to outlier	8/9/2011 18:15	8/9/2011 18:15	9/12/2011 14:35	1
EStarkey	Delete point(s)- due to outlier	8/10/2011 19:15	8/10/2011 19:15	9/12/2011 14:36	1
EStarkey	Delete point(s)- due to outlier	8/20/2011 9:15	8/20/2011 9:15	9/12/2011 14:37	1
EStarkey	Delete point(s)- due to outlier	8/21/2011 13:15	8/21/2011 13:15	9/12/2011 14:37	1
EStarkey	Delete point(s)- due to outlier	8/22/2011 3:15	8/22/2011 3:15	9/12/2011 14:38	1
EStarkey	Delete Region- due to outliers and suspect data	8/5/2011 7:15	8/5/2011 8:15	9/12/2011 14:42	2
EStarkey	Delete point(s)- due to outlier	9/9/2011 1:00	9/9/2011 1:00	9/26/2011 14:27	1
EStarkey	Delete Region- due to outlier	9/10/2011 12:00	9/10/2011 12:00	9/26/2011 14:27	1
EStarkey	Delete Region- due to outlier	9/11/2011 7:00	9/11/2011 7:00	9/26/2011 14:27	1
EStarkey	Delete Region- due to outlier	9/16/2011 8:00	9/16/2011 8:00	9/26/2011 14:28	1
EStarkey	Delete Region- due to outlier	9/18/2011 0:00	9/18/2011 0:00	9/26/2011 14:28	1
EStarkey	Delete Region- due to outlier	9/18/2011 12:00	9/18/2011 13:00	9/26/2011 14:28	2
EStarkey	Drift Correction with Calibration Drift value of 20.05NTU and Fouling Drift value of 0.00NTU	8/24/2011 16:00	9/22/2011 11:00	9/26/2011 14:32	685
EStarkey	Delete Region- due to outlier	9/24/2011 9:30	9/24/2011 9:30	10/31/2011 13:07	1
EStarkey	Delete Region- due to outlier	9/26/2011 20:30	9/26/2011 20:30	10/31/2011 13:07	1
EStarkey	Delete Region- due to outlier	9/27/2011 3:30	9/27/2011 3:30	10/31/2011 13:07	1

Appendix E. Corrections History (continued)

Correction history for Mill Creek, WHMI 2011 turbidity data (continued).

Creator	Comment	From Time	To Time	Applied Time	Points Modified
EStarkey	Delete Region- due to outlier	9/30/2011 9:30	9/30/2011 9:30	10/31/2011 13:08	1
EStarkey	Delete point(s)- due to outlier	10/4/2011 3:30	10/4/2011 3:30	10/31/2011 13:09	1
EStarkey	Delete point(s)- due to outlier	10/13/2011 18:30	10/13/2011 18:30	10/31/2011 13:10	1
EStarkey	Delete point(s)- due to outlier	10/19/2011 4:30	10/19/2011 4:30	10/31/2011 13:10	1

Appendix F. Macroinvertebrate Metrics

NPS Upper Columbia Basin Benthos 2011 – WHMI
*Standardized to OTU and fixed count

SampleID	147161	147162
Station (NAMC)	PIBO:3194	PIBO:3195
Station (Customer)	6460	6461
Waterbody	Mill	Doan
County	Walla Walla	Walla Walla
State	WA	WA
Latitude	46.04218851	46.04414805
Longitude	-118.4687082	-118.4604884
Collection Date	8/2/2011	8/3/2011
Habitat Sampled	Targeted Riffle	Targeted Riffle
Collection Method	Surber Net	Surber Net
Field Notes	NULL	NULL
Lab Notes	NULL	NULL
Area sampled (m^2)	0.74	0.74
Field Split	100	100
Lab Split	15.63	100
Split Count	626	80
Fixed Count	300	78
Big Rare Count	10	0
Richness*	21	8
Abundance	5426	108
Shannon's Diversity*	1.922089316	1.564579855
Simpson's Diversity*	0.731103679	0.738594739
Evenness*	0.631327033	0.752403866
# of EPT Taxa*	9	1
EPT Taxa Abundance	2047	7
Dominant Family	Chironomidae	
Abundance of Dominant Family	2640	47
Dominant Taxa	Orthocladiinae	Oligochaeta
Abundance of Dominant Taxa	2060	46
Hilsenhoff Biotic Index*	4.16	2.5
# of Intolerant Taxa*	2	1
Intolerant Taxa abundance	158	7
# of Tolerant Taxa*	0	1
Tolerant Taxa abundance	9	1
USFS Community Tolerance Quotient (d)*	88	96
# of shredder taxa*	2	1
Shredder Abundance	61	7

Appendix F. Macroinvertebrate Metrics (continued)

NPS Upper Columbia Basin Benthos 2011 – WHMI
*Standardized to OTU and fixed count

SampleID	147161	147162
Station (NAMC)	PIBO:3194	PIBO:3195
Station (Customer)	6460	6461
Waterbody	Mill	Doan
County	Walla Walla	Walla Walla
State	WA	WA
Latitude	46.04218851	46.04414805
Longitude	-118.4687082	-118.4604884
Collection Date	8/2/2011	8/3/2011
Habitat Sampled	Targeted Riffle	Targeted Riffle
Collection Method	Surber Net	Surber Net
# of scraper taxa*	1	0
Scraper abundance	131	0
# of collector-filterer taxa*	1	0
Collector-filterer abundance	1399	1
# of collector-gatherer taxa*	10	6
Collector-gatherer abundance	3239	100
# of predator taxa*	2	1
Predator abundance	493	0
# of clinger taxa*	5	0
Long-lived Taxa*	4	0
# of Ephemeroptera taxa*	4	0
Ephemeroptera abundance	519	0
# of Plecoptera taxa*	0	0
Plecoptera abundance	9	0
# of Trichoptera taxa*	5	1
Trichoptera abundance	1520	7
# of Coleoptera taxa*	3	0
Coleoptera abundance	131	0
# of Elmidae Taxa*	3	0
Elmidae abundance	121	0
# of Megaloptera taxa*	0	0
Megaloptera abundance	0	0
# of Diptera taxa*	5	2
Diptera abundance	2674	41
# of Chironomidae taxa*	3	2
Chironomidae abundance	2640	39
# of Crustacea taxa*	0	0
Crustacea abundance	0	0

Appendix F. Macroinvertebrate Metrics (continued)

NPS Upper Columbia Basin Benthos 2011 – WHMI
*Standardized to OTU and fixed count

SampleID	147161	147162
Station (NAMC)	PIBO:3194	PIBO:3195
Station (Customer)	6460	6461
Waterbody	Mill	Doan
County	Walla Walla	Walla Walla
State	WA	WA
Latitude	46.04218851	46.04414805
Longitude	-118.4687082	-118.4604884
Collection Date	8/2/2011	8/3/2011
Habitat Sampled	Targeted Riffle	Targeted Riffle
Collection Method	Surber Net	Surber Net
# of Oligochaete taxa*	0	0
Oligochaete abundance	0	46
# of Mollusca taxa*	1	1
Mollusca abundance	9	8
# of Insect taxa*	18	3
Insect abundance	4939	47
# of Non-insect taxa*	3	5
Non-insect abundance	487	61

Appendix G. Macroinvertebrate Taxa List

NPS Upper Columbia Basin Benthos 2011 – WHMI
Note that all samples were from targeted riffles and sampled using Surber nets.

SAMPLE	STATION	NAME	SAMPDATE	LAB SPLIT	AREA	TSN	CODE	TAXON	Split Count	Big Rare Count	DENSITY (#/m2)
147162	PIBO:3195	Doan	8/3/2011	100	0.74	68422	19	Oligochaeta	34	0	46
147162	PIBO:3195	Doan	8/3/2011	100	0.74	93294	69	Amphipoda	1	0	1
147162	PIBO:3195	Doan	8/3/2011	100	0.74	93773	71	Gammarus	2	0	3
147162	PIBO:3195	Doan	8/3/2011	100	0.74	94025	75	Hyalella	1	0	1
147162	PIBO:3195	Doan	8/3/2011	100	0.74	116794	519	Lepidostoma	5	0	7
147162	PIBO:3195	Doan	8/3/2011	100	0.74	126640	221	Simuliidae	1	0	1
147162	PIBO:3195	Doan	8/3/2011	100	0.74	128457	184	Orthocladiinae	16	0	22
147162	PIBO:3195	Doan	8/3/2011	100	0.74	129228	182	Chironominae	13	0	18
147162	PIBO:3195	Doan	8/3/2011	100	0.74	167229	1226	Cottus	1	0	1
147162	PIBO:3195	Doan	8/3/2011	100	0.74	76677	610	Physa	6	0	8
147161	PIBO:3194	Mill	8/2/2011	15.63	0.74	76677	610	Physa	1	0	9
147161	PIBO:3194	Mill	8/2/2011	15.63	0.74	82769	58	Trombidiformes	18	0	156
147161	PIBO:3194	Mill	8/2/2011	15.63	0.74	83005	66	Sperchonidae	25	0	216
147161	PIBO:3194	Mill	8/2/2011	15.63	0.74	100801	907	Acentrella	4	0	35
147161	PIBO:3194	Mill	8/2/2011	15.63	0.74	114070	170	Psephenus	1	1	10
147161	PIBO:3194	Mill	8/2/2011	15.63	0.74	114236	1077	Ordobrevia nubifera	2	0	17
147161	PIBO:3194	Mill	8/2/2011	15.63	0.74	115398	495	Hydropsychidae	89	0	769
147161	PIBO:3194	Mill	8/2/2011	15.63	0.74	115453	499	Hydropsyche	59	3	514
147161	PIBO:3194	Mill	8/2/2011	15.63	0.74	115629	506	Hydroptilidae	3	0	26
147161	PIBO:3194	Mill	8/2/2011	15.63	0.74	116794	519	Lepidostoma	4	0	35
147161	PIBO:3194	Mill	8/2/2011	15.63	0.74	127994	187	Tanypodinae	9	0	78
147161	PIBO:3194	Mill	8/2/2011	15.63	0.74	135830	200	Empididae	2	0	17
147161	PIBO:3194	Mill	8/2/2011	15.63	0.74	136352	2253	Neoplasta	1	0	9
147161	PIBO:3194	Mill	8/2/2011	15.63	0.74	53964	655	Turbellaria	0	1	1
147161	PIBO:3194	Mill	8/2/2011	15.63	0.74	93773	71	Gammarus	12	1	105

Appendix G. Macroinvertebrate Taxa List (continued)

NPS Upper Columbia Basin Benthos 2011 – WHMI
Note that all samples were from targeted riffles and sampled using Surber nets.

SAMPLE	STATION	NAME	SAMPDATE	LAB SPLIT	AREA	TSN	CODE	TAXON	Split Count	Big Rare Count	DENSITY (#/m2)
147161	PIBO:3194	Mill	8/2/2011	15.63	0.74	100755	249	Baetidae	31	0	268
147161	PIBO:3194	Mill	8/2/2011	15.63	0.74	100800	250	Baetis	3	0	26
147161	PIBO:3194	Mill	8/2/2011	15.63	0.74	101405	307	Tricorythodes	18	0	156
147161	PIBO:3194	Mill	8/2/2011	15.63	0.74	102077	374	Coenagrionidae	1	0	9
147161	PIBO:3194	Mill	8/2/2011	15.63	0.74	103102	469	Skwala	1	0	9
147161	PIBO:3194	Mill	8/2/2011	15.63	0.74	114093	121	Elmidae	4	0	35
147161	PIBO:3194	Mill	8/2/2011	15.63	0.74	114130	1751	Dubiraphia quadrinotata	1	0	9
147161	PIBO:3194	Mill	8/2/2011	15.63	0.74	114177	135	Optioservus	5	0	43
147161	PIBO:3194	Mill	8/2/2011	15.63	0.74	114180	1076	Optioservus quadrimaculatus	2	0	17
147161	PIBO:3194	Mill	8/2/2011	15.63	0.74	115095	480	Trichoptera	4	0	35
147161	PIBO:3194	Mill	8/2/2011	15.63	0.74	116651	522	Nectopsyche	3	0	26
147161	PIBO:3194	Mill	8/2/2011	15.63	0.74	116918	932	Brachycentrus occidentalis	13	2	115
147161	PIBO:3194	Mill	8/2/2011	15.63	0.74	117682	350	Petrophila	9	0	78
147161	PIBO:3194	Mill	8/2/2011	15.63	0.74	119660	236	Antocha monticola	1	0	9
147161	PIBO:3194	Mill	8/2/2011	15.63	0.74	127917	180	Chironomidae	15	0	130
147161	PIBO:3194	Mill	8/2/2011	15.63	0.74	128457	184	Orthocladiinae	238	2	2060
147161	PIBO:3194	Mill	8/2/2011	15.63	0.74	129228	182	Chironominae	43	0	372
147161	PIBO:3194	Mill	8/2/2011	15.63	0.74	568601	1407	Fallceon quilleri	4	0	35

NPS 371/114303, June 2012